UNDATEABLE.

BOBBY SHANKS

UNDATEABLE

Printed and Electronic Versions
ISBN   978-1-956353-04-4
(Bobby Shanks/Motivation Champs)

The book was printed
in the United States of America.

Special discount may apply on bulk quantities.
Please contact Motivation Champs Publishing to order.
www.motivationchamps.com

DISCLAIMER

The stories in this book reflect the author's recollection of events. Some names, locations, identifying characteristics and specifics have been changed for the purpose of this book and to protect the privacy of those depicted. Dialogues have been re-created from memory.

Contents

DEDICATION

Kogan, my amazing and awesome son! I love you with all my heart and could write a book on so many things that are of vital importance for a young man beginning life's journey. I chose to write this book and its topics and suggestions above all other things. What I've learned from years of relationships in business, my personal life, and marriage is this: Who you choose to co-pilot life's journey with will be the single most-important decision you'll ever make. It will have effects on your life greater and of more importance than anything else you'll ever do or that will ever happen to you. When you choose the right person as your mate, it will enrich and bless your life beyond your wildest dreams. It will even catapult you beyond the realm of your own abilities. The opposite is also true: If you choose the wrong person, it can cause nothing short of emotional, physical, and economic paralysis from which, if corrective action isn't taken, you will live a life of utter resentment, disappointment, and fear. Choose wisely, my son.

CHAPTER 1

Why Singles Today Are Undateable

Singles have become undateable: 18, 21, 33, 45, '50s, '60s—all of us that identify as being in the "single" category. If you're married and contemplating divorce, I want to seriously encourage you to try counseling first. Why? Because if you think your marriage has its dark sides—whatever they are—trust me, being single has just as many, if not more. I know what you're thinking: This guy is bitter, divorced, middle aged, and calloused. That's why he is undateable. On the contrary, I'm a pretty upbeat and positive person. I love people, all people. I love going on dates, and I am open to a variety of prospective dating opportunities. But what I (and millions of others) have found is that once I get to a certain point—let's call it the D.T.R. (determine the relationship)—in the dating process, I tend to fizzle because I clearly see that the person I'm dating isn't a suitable long-term solution. Or, just as likely to happen, I can see that I am not suitable for them. I'm not sure which is the chicken and which is the egg, but the outcome is the same: a soggy, undercooked egg that I'm sorry to say is on its way to the trash can after only a couple of dates. So why have singles today become undateable?

There are a myriad of reasons (and not enough pages in this book) to fully cover them all, but I'm going to venture ahead and outline some of the reasons why and even carefully describe some of my own experiences.

First, a quick overview about me. Afterall, in this day and age, you have to know who you're dealing with when it comes to such commentary. As of this writing, I'm forty-five years old. I've been married twice. The first marriage was a success. Yes, you read that right. It was a successful marriage because we were married for a long time, had two kids, owned a couple of homes, had careers, were good parents, and by all definitions, we were doing the right things. Ultimately the marriage ended simply because from day one we just weren't compatible. We were "in love" with our commitment to the marriage, but sadly, we just weren't "in love" with each other. On paper, we were the perfect power couple! We both had good jobs, dressed the part, had nice homes, cars, friends, went to church, voted, active in our community, and more. We were the model of a good marriage. Behind closed doors, we just weren't interested in the same things, or each other. For the most part, we were great parents. Other than that, we just didn't have "it!" We weren't soul mates; we weren't best friends; we didn't make decisions together; we just thought on different levels. Neither of us were completely right, and neither of us were completely wrong. We just existed.

In my very brief second marriage, it was the opposite of my first marriage. We were completely compatible; we had the same interests; we loved kids; we were madly in love with each other, and we had excellent communication. It ended because ultimately we just weren't on the same page with our "style" of raising children, and we had a blended family of six kids. Word to the wise, if you're blending families, just know that "parenting" will become the marriage, and it will be the hardest chasm to cross. Plus, the more kids there are, the harder it will be.

On a personal level, and probably like many of you reading this now, I feel that I'm very desirable in today's dating pool. I'm tall, have an athletic build, relatively smart, own a business, have a college degree, and heck, I even have straight white teeth. I know how to treat a gal the right way, and I'm fun to be with! Plus, I actually do like to go out and have fun—whether it's dinner and a movie, travel, winery on a Sunday, motorcycle riding, hitting the gym, or really just about anything. So why then do I perceive that I'm undateable . . . like so many others?

You know how people often say, "Well, that's a simple enough question to answer?" Let me assure you: Anyone that's single today—whether they're actively pursuing a relationship or not—will resoundingly admit that either they themselves or those they've tried dating are undateable. Therefore, the answer to this dilemma simply isn't simple!

The first consideration is that we live in a society today where focusing on a career and/or the right education to pursue a career is almost always the number one goal and is perceived as the right path to ultimate happiness. Regardless of whether you're pursuing a high-paying career or a job that's more simplistic and straightforward, in our world today the "pursuit of happiness" comes with the price tag of long hours, difficult competition with others, and the need to constantly hone one's professional skills to climb the ladder of success. Even if you're a work-from-home mom, dad, or someone that doesn't receive an actual paycheck, you are constantly chasing this almost-unattainable level of perfection and achievement.

Underneath this never-ending chase of striving to feel adequate at our work is the constant bombardment of perfect-role-model mannequins presented to all of us on social media of what we should look like, behave like, eat like, talk like, and more. For example, in at least the last twenty-plus years there has been this tremendous focus on what images our young girls are seeing in the media. Is there really such a thing as a real-life Barbie, and is it what you should be striving for if you're an adolescent woman maturing into adulthood?

While this focus has been primarily on young females, that is only the beginning. What about young boys maturing into men? These days, they not only have to be strong, handsome, and handy around the house, they also have to be experts at computers, flow charts, navigating corporate job politics, and strong leaders. At the same time, we expect them to be quiet, calm, and firmly in touch with their feminine side. Right?

In these two simple gender examples, I spelled out just two of society's traditional stereotypes. But in each example, the inverse is also true: Our girls are expected to become as financially independent as their male counterparts—blazing their way to their own financial well-being while at the same time fixing their own leaky toilets, changing tires, cutting grass, and living by the motto, "If he can do it, I can do it." The same is true for boys becoming men: Bake your own pie from scratch, learn to sew, do laundry, and know how to do all things a woman can do so you don't end up selecting a woman that can do things for you rather than one that is right for you.

Here's the problem and the ultimate answer as to why singles are undateable: We've been raised and have learned to become so self-sufficient that we simply don't need a mate to function in life. We are a team of one!

Here's the problem and the ultimate answer as to why singles are undateable: We've been raised and have learned to become so self-sufficient that we simply don't need a mate to function in life. We are a team of one! Advancements in work neutrality, equal pay for equal work, organized religion, self-help books, podcasts, social media, politics and, most certainly, technology have vastly enabled these behaviors in all genders. Yes, I went plural on ya there, to the simple truth that a person of any gender today can satisfy all their needs in life (even the need to be self-fulfilled intimately) without the complications and friction that a committed monogamous relationship offers. Need more proof? Think about your parents and your grandparents. On the average, baby-boom couples are vastly more self-sufficient as individual people than their parents from the Great Depression, and even your great-grandparents from the early 1900s, compared to your grandparents.

As with all societies throughout time, there is a natural evolution to the human dynamic, and it is spurred forward generation by generation, a little at a time. But the speed of this evolution as it relates to mated pairs increases at a growing rate the more advanced we become with technology, mechanics, physical and mental health, and life longevity, just to name a few. For centuries, couples existed to have children, and there were very definable gender-based roles inside the family unit. Today, we don't have to have kids to help run the family farm or business, and because of gender equality in the workplace, you don't even have to be coupled for financial reasons. We have become a generation of singles that seek the perfect soul mate to pursue only happiness. Everything else is second.

But there's a huge problem with this modern-day pursuit of relationship happiness. Your so-called soul mate that you're wanting to ride off into the sunset with ultimately isn't going to make you happy, even if you've convinced yourself you've found that one true love. Only you can decide to be happy. Think about the thousands of inspirational memes you've read in the past decade on social media about "true love" and finding your "soul mate." How many of those memes talked about tolerance, forgiveness, communication about sex, being a united front as parents, or even putting others before yourself? Not many! Most are anecdotal fluffy, white cotton-ball clouds about saying "I love you" before bed each night or remembering to make dating an active part of your marriage, or better yet, "Make yourself happy first," and which zodiac sign is the most compatible with yours.

Look, I'm not knocking any of this stuff, but the reality is that there is so much more to being dateable. When you read all this crap over and over, day in and day out, you can't help but be overwhelmingly influenced by it to the point that you become, well, undateable, because your perception of Mr. Right, Ms. Right, or even the "right" version of yourself, becomes so skewed you can't even figure yourself out. So guess what happens? The result is that the path of least resistance is to just be perfect for yourself, all by yourself. When you reach that perfect level of enlightenment, God or Karma, or whatever you believe in, is going to all of a sudden drop the perfect-for-you person in your life. Tell me I'm wrong. I dare you!

Literally, just now, as I'm writing this chapter, I received a Tweet from one of the most well-known podcasters in the world today: the infamous and all-knowing Gary Vaynerchuk himself. His Tweet simply reads, "What can you send you?" followed by two red heart emojis. Ha! Talk about the right timing! What the heck, Vaynerchuk? What am I supposed to do, send myself my favorite bottle of whiskey to remind myself how much I love me? I listen to podcasts from Gary Vaynerchuk, Grant Cardone, Rachel Hollis, Andy Frisella, and countless others (I have for years now), and the one thing they all have in common is this: If it is to be, it is up to me!

I want to send a clear message about all of these self-help books and podcasts: They're 100 percent correct when they say you have to do "self-work" in order to become the best version of yourself—although I think that phrase is a bit overused and it would be better to say "Make an improved version of yourself" instead. If you want to be strong, you gotta lift. If you want to be healthy, you gotta eat right. If you want to be smart, you gotta read. But I also believe that you can become so magnificent that you basically don't leave any room for someone else in your life if they're not at your level. Worse yet, if you seek out that equally magnificent counterpart, guess what? Two negatives may make a positive in math, but two positives don't always equal the ultimate positive. There are no absolutes one way or another. Literature is full of examples of successful people, couples, business partners and the like, where those people were very similar in some cases and yet in others they were polar opposites.

So what's the point of all this hubbub I'm rambling on about? It's simply this: if you want to live happily ever after all by your single self, then go for it. And if you want to attract the right mate, then you gotta let go of the notion that you're undateable, and read the following chapters. To achieve the realization that while you may be self-sufficient in every way imaginable, that level you've reached in life isn't going to cuddle you at night to warm your cold feet or wipe your tears when your mom passes away. It's also not gonna tell you what a great job you did on the black diamond slope on the best vacation of your life. Oh yeah, one more thing: It's not gonna give you the best dang orgasm you've had this week either—take my word for it—but you already know that!

Even if you're convinced that you're undateable and destined to be single forever, this book is perfect for you. If you're married and your overzealous spouse roped you into reading this together to rekindle some old flames and get things back to "the good ole days," go for it, because this book is for you too. Being "undateable" is a phenomenon that affects married couples just as much as it does singles.

Lastly, if you're a hopeless romantic single like me, and you refuse to give up the ambition to find that less-than-perfect but perfect-for-you person to add value to your life, then this book is most definitely for you.

CHAPTER 2

Are You Available?

There is so much to unpack about this notion that we've become a society of single undateable people and, worse yet, a society of married couples that have forgotten how to date the person we love, cherish, and have devoted our life to. I've written this book backwards; that is, I'm going to attempt to hit the home run on the first pitch; and here it is in this very simple question: Are you available?

Notice I didn't ask "Are you attractive?" "Are you smart?" "Do you have a job?" "Do you have your life together?" There is no question more urgent to answer than whether or not you're available to date so that you can get to know another person in the hopes that you are a match for them and they are a match for you. Remember that phrase I mentioned earlier, "If it is to be, it is up to me." That is so true as it relates to your availability.

As of the time of this writing, I'm a self-described, successful midwestern real estate agent with a nice home in the suburbs of St. Louis. I have three children and two that live at home with me and split time between my place and their mom's, equally. At least nine months out of the year I work seven days a week, and that includes a lot of nights and other odd hours. I'm actively involved in my community, charity, church, and even serve as a trustee for my subdivision. I go to the gym five days a week for about ninety minutes. I'm a writer and very active on nearly all social media platforms both for professional and personal purposes. I shop, cook, clean, decorate, grill, entertain, and do all the things that normal married couples share responsibility doing; and I do it very well. I also don't complain about it, as I enjoy all my responsibilities and obligations. It's my life, I'm happy with it, and I work hard at everything I do. I have lost count of the dozens upon dozens of times I've heard someone say to me, "How in the hell do you manage all that?" Oh yeah, one more very important thing—I date! Not only do I date, but I actively date, not passively. What I mean is I look for opportunities to date, I pursue the date, I show up for the date, and I perpetuate a dating relationship when I think it makes sense.

To answer the question, "How in the hell do I have time for all of this," my answer is simple: I make time. I'm available morning, noon, night, weekdays, and weekends. I make it work, however and whenever. Yes, it's hard, and it doesn't always work out perfectly. I have a golden rule both in my personal life and in my professional life: If it's in my calendar, I make it happen. For those of you who manage your life without a calendar, I applaud you, and I am in awe. I simply don't have that ability nor do I have the memory to function that way. By and large, most people have a calendar on their smartphone these days and actively use it. If you're single, wish to date, and simply don't have time, then I'm afraid I have to set the record straight here: You have time. You're just not managing it in a way that makes time for you to date.

So how much time do you need to transition yourself from undateable to dateable? Only you can answer that question, but trust me, you have the time. Now, if you're in a challenging spot in your life due to workload, family responsibilities, caring for a special-needs person or some other challenging circumstance, then that's understandable. As my good ole mom has said numerous times in my life during my life's struggles, "This too shall pass." Not having time to date "right now" isn't the same thing as not having time ever. It's been my vast experience in many things in life that what you focus on is what expands in your life around you. If your focus is money, then you'll get it. If your focus is God, then you'll be closer to your Maker than ever. If your focus is paying off debt, then you'll achieve it. And if your focus is to date and have that companion in your life, then you'll have it.

The biggest challenge I've heard from singles these days is the frustration with dating, the letdowns, the waste of time they perceive it is. If you believe you're wasting your time by continuing to date, then yes, you certainly are undateable. Dating isn't a waste of time; it's an investment. It's an investment in yourself and in someone else. Whatever investment you're able to make in dating, do it in earnest, do it with intention, and do it with positivity. The minute you get negative about the process, it becomes "unfun" and discouraging. You will most certainly perceive it as a waste of time. Think about other goals you've set for yourself in the past and attained them: Was that an investment or a begrudging and barely tolerable existence? It was an investment, right? When you reached your goal, it was worth it in the end, right? Of course it was! Was it hard? Of course. Did you have to make some sacrifices? Of course. Did you reach a new level of enlightenment, education, self improvement, and sense of fulfillment? Hell yes! Dating is no different! What you focus on expands, and it does so only when you do it with the right mindset, positivity, and never-say-die attitude.

In contract law, there is a term called "Time is of the essence." What it means is that once a contract is agreed upon, all parties have a contractual duty to perform on the terms of the contract within a certain amount of time. If a party doesn't perform according to the terms of the contract, that party is in "breach." Then the poo hits the fan. While this is a fundamental reality in all forms of business and institutions, there is definitely not a boilerplate contract to turn to in the dating world. Honestly, that's one reason why so many people are undateable, because they have this skewed belief system that there is a defined path for dating. Kind of like the old nursery rhyme about two kids sitting in a tree singing "First comes love, then comes marriage, then comes baby in a baby carriage." Funny, right? That's not dating, and that's definitely not modern-day relationships for singles or monogamous relationships, whether they're married or not.

If you feel that you're undateable, one reason might be because you have an old-fashioned view of what the dating path looks like. There is no perfectly defined timeline. There is no right way to "do dating" for the masses of single people. Performance in dating doesn't follow a "Time is of the essence" timeline, so once and for all, rid yourself of that notion.

If you feel that you're undateable, one reason might be because you have an old-fashioned view of what the dating path looks like. There is no perfectly defined timeline. There is no right way to "do dating" for the masses of single people. Performance in dating doesn't follow a "Time is of the essence" timeline, so once and for all, rid yourself of that notion. If you want to kiss someone on the first date rather than waiting for the third date, then go for it. If you don't want to kiss someone until the one-month mark or only after you have the "religion" conversation, then do that. The only thing that has to work is for the other person to be in agreement. If they're not in agreement with your standard, then great, it's time to move on. But keep in mind, there are big things and there are little things for every individual. What's a big thing for you might be of little thought to the person you're wanting to date or are actively dating.

One thing I've learned time and time again—both the right way and the wrong way—is the best time to communicate is RIGHT NOW. But first you have to have a man/woman-in-the-mirror moment and know exactly what you want, seek that out, communicate about it, don't make any assumptions about the other person's reaction, and be intentional with the standards you're setting for yourself and the other person. Once you communicate, you can't "uncrack" that egg, so be sure of yourself. For the record, being intentional doesn't mean writing out your dating resume and taking a printed copy on your first date—although I could actually see that working in some instances!

Listen, this is serious business. You must "know thyself" before you can even make a mental list of your three pillars and your second list of three bonus things. You must consider the context of your list given where you are in life, your current state of affairs, and your age. What's really important to you right now might not be that important this time next year or in twenty years. So do you want to date the perfect person for you right now or the perfect person for you over the next twenty years? This is one of those moments where you might actually want to stop reading, grab a pen, and jot your thoughts in the margin. If you're listening to this book via audio and you're driving, hit the pause button and make a mental list to write in your planner or on a sticky note to put on your monitor or bathroom mirror later. Record yourself using a text message to send to yourself. I can't stress how important this is. Are your three pillars a reflection of where you are "right now" or are these the all-important, deep-rooted things in your psyche and your personality that you simply cannot bend on—not ever, for the rest of your life? Men, on average, will undoubtedly label sex as a hot item. Women will write sex only as a single bullet point, in addition to a long list of others that they'll have to choose from—then change their mind multiple times. Ladies, it's okay if sex doesn't make the list of your top three. Men, it's totally normal if sex not only makes your top three list but is unabashedly the number one spot on the list. Male or female, you only need three big ones to complete this exercise. What's your list?

I've dated enough to write this book. Maybe I haven't been single for years and years, but I'm a quick study. The fact that I've spent so much of my adult life married also gives me a leg up on modern-day dating. Like many of you reading this now, I'm divorced. Twice. Gulp! As a real estate agent, I work in a woman-dominated industry and have a massive amount of insight about women—not to mention that in my area of expertise, residential real estate, a vast majority of the decision makers regarding home purchasing are women. I am surrounded by women as coworkers and as clients; and most of my closest friends, you guessed it, are women. All of this combined has blessed me with a knowledge base about women and has adequately prepared me for dating. At least, that's what I thought!

Ms. Treadmill

I met this gal years ago at the gym. While walking on the treadmill, from time to time we talked and developed a conversational friendship. There was never any funny business at all, just good ole conversation. I thought about asking her out but just never pulled the trigger. Meanwhile, I did start dating the woman that eventually became my second wife. We got married, and that was the end of Ms. Treadmill.

After my very brief second marriage ended in divorce, I struck up a conversation with Ms. Treadmill online. It was short, totally casual, and not flirty at all. She suggested that we should go out sometime. Oh boy! Okay, it was time for me to make a decision if I wanted to go out with this gal or just be pals. Being somewhat newly single, I thought to myself, "What the heck, I like this gal," so we went out on a date.

We met up at a popular restaurant, drank some wine, ate some food, and had a very stimulating and flirtatious conversation. This gal was very intelligent, very beautiful, very much at my intellectual level, and very amorous. We were a match on most levels. However, there was a problem, and the problem was with me!

It started to rain as we left the restaurant and ended up in the front seat of my vehicle to have more conversation. Truly what was about to happen was totally a surprise to both of us. We had that semi-awkward moment of silence. You know, that moment where it's about to get really awesome or the date is over and it's time to say goodnight. I looked at her in that silent moment and said, "I really want to kiss you." Yes, I know that's so cheesy, but you had to be there. Trust me, it was perfect. This wasn't the type of girl you took chances on or just swung the bat with your eyes closed. Her response was perfect. She said, "Why don't you!" It was on! We locked lips for a solid ten minutes right there in the front seat of my truck, and it was spectacular. That's as far as it went!

Ladies, you know those awesome tingles you get after a great date. Like, who's going to text whom first before you get home and then stay up until 2:00 a.m. just texting and laughing. Then it's followed by the next date, then another. Yeah, that's not this story. I'm afraid I was the other guy, the jerk that didn't text to make sure you got home okay. And I didn't even call the next day. In fact, I didn't call at all. Ergggg! Sorry, ladies. Please don't hate me, rip the book in half, and burn me an effigy. Oh, and sorry to you, too, Ms. Treadmill. You are the bomb.com, and you know that!

As I implied above, the problem was with me. I really liked this girl, a lot. She was awesome. She was accomplished, smart, stunning, and totally had her life together—this is totally the twenty-plus-year type of girl! The problem was that I just didn't "feel it." Ok, ok, ok, ladies, I know you really hate me now. I know what you're thinking: *So why the hell did you lead her on like that?*

And if you figured out that you didn't "feel it," why couldn't you just call her and be a man about it? Well, those are great questions. They are the right questions. The answer is this: While I know a lot about women and what makes them tick, I'm still a dude working on my dating game. I just chickened out. One day of silence on my part turned into three, then a week, then a month. Eventually, she initiated contact with me, and we talked about it. She was so grown up about it. She was very communicative and made it clear that what I did was wrong. I'm definitely not sorry about the hot make-out session, but not following up with her about my change of heart was totally a bad move and one that I'll never repeat.

Ms. Superwoman

She was a ten—no, she was a twenty. She was blonde and indescribably—no, dangerously gorgeous, and had big red lips that once you started staring at them you couldn't stop. She had a firm and fit body, juicy ass, and breasts that were perfectly sized and shaped. She was as equally comfortable in camo clothes and a ball cap as she was in an ultra-tight bright red cocktail dress with gleaming ruby red high heels. Men want her and women want to be her. She was a business owner, owned real estate, made a ton of money and, next to the word "mom" in the dictionary was her name and pictures and pages describing how incredible she was at motherhood. She had high standards, values, was street smart, and a total badass! She was crafty, a great cook, loved to drink beer, and loved doing "guy stuff" outdoors. She was, in a word, a "unicorn!" She worked a lot. Like, a lot! When she wasn't working, she was very busy with other normal-life things that we all have as single people, and she took her parenting very seriously. This fine specimen of an all-American woman did not do anything passively. She was definitely my equal on all levels!

So, where did I fit into this equation? Well, not as much as I would have liked. The first time we dated we actually spent quite a bit of time together. She worked at it and so did I. All of this happened during the COVID-19 pandemic. Work was slow for both of us. Once the world started to come back online, it got really tough. We were totally into each other, me perhaps a little more than her. Scheduling was brutal, and we spent less and less time together. The horrific thing is that we only lived ten minutes apart. Our tough schedules combined with having similar personality traits (both type A) ended things rather abruptly. So we took some time off and tried again weeks later, again with the same result.

We are still friends today. And I don't know about her, but she's the girl I often think to myself that maybe in the future things will be different. Probably not, but she's a magnificent gal, and I'm only human. It's hard not to think about her.

Let's glue this together now. Are you available? If you're going to take dating seriously and rid yourself of the notion that you're undateable, then yes, you are available. Close your eyes and say it out loud, "I'm available!" Make time for it. Schedule it. What you focus on expands. If you focus on having the time for dating, then I promise you, dating opportunities are going to show up in your universe. Have faith in this process. It works. Next, know what your big three must-haves are from dating that special person you seek and stick to those standards as you venture out.

Don't do what I did in my first personal anecdote. Knowing what your big-three items are means sticking to them and not leading someone on hoping they'll magically appear later—whether it's time together or your big-three items.

My dating advice is this: A little kiss good night is totally cool, but making out with someone (or more) that you know you have no future with is harmful and a waste of time. Know your big three and communicate those things. Do so in a fun, considerate, and "do no harm" sort of way. You're an adult: Trust your gut. You'll figure this out and get better as you go.

CHAPTER 3

The Three Pillars

Your "Three Pillars" are related to your core values. I know a lot of people reading this are strong faith-based people, and they will want to sum up their three pillars into one: "Does this person have the same beliefs as me?" or "Does this person believe in Jesus and is a Christian?" That's awesome and an important start, but there's more. If you're starting your Three Pillars list with a religious stance, keep in mind that divorce statistics for believers versus nonbelievers are pretty much the same; that is, around 50 percent of first-time-married couples end in divorce. The divorce rate for second and third marriages is over 60 percent.

Roll your sleeves up and let's get to work on your three pillars. What are your core values and what or where do they stem from? Is it from your childhood? Is it the way you were raised? Do you frame your thinking based upon your parents' or grandparents' marriage? Are those role-model relationships positive or negative? I want you to think like this: If you were on a deserted island for the remainder of your days, all alone, just you and nature, what would be your core values? If you were Truman from the movie *The Truman Show* and all the world watched you on your deserted island for years, and even decades, what would people say were your core values? Write them here.

1.

2.

3.

Got it? Excellent job! You're on your way to meeting the right person because you now know in your heart what makes you "you!" Next, let's make sure that what you wrote is truly chiseled down to its perfect marble statue form that will be who you are now, tomorrow, and for the remainder of your days—and even what your grandkids will know you by.

Is making your bed each morning a core value? I know that's a silly example, but let's use it as a template to overlay a thought process on what you wrote above. Why do you make your bed each morning? What happens if you don't? Are you dead to the world that day or incapable of thinking about anything else, rendering yourself useless to yourself and others? Probably not. So what is it then? When you make your bed each morning, what does that do for you? Does it give you a sense of accomplishment knowing you've completed one simple task that day, and further, that you've primed your engine to complete many more with increasing complexity? Do you do it because you know that you love that feeling of sliding into smooth, cold sheets at night and how it calms you and puts you right to sleep? In your ideal relationship, would that other person share the duty of making the bed on an equal rotation? What if that other person couldn't care less and has never made their bed a day in their life; would you harbor resentment or would you truck along making the bed every day as usual because it's what you need for your own fulfillment? Take a deep breath, channel your inner Zen, and ask yourself, "Is this a core value? Does it define me to my core?" You should also ask the questions, "Am I this person; will I be this person; and will I do this activity forever?" If your answer is "Yes," then you've nailed it. I often find at these moments of deep introspective solitude that a few more firm swings with the hammer on the chisel will refine this statue into its true and intended detail.

Are your Three Pillars in harmony with each other? Does one complement the other two, and vice versa? Are they equal and balanced or is one lesser than the other two? Think of these big three as an equilateral triangle laying flat and carefully placed on a center post; does it balance?

Are your Three Pillars in harmony with each other? Does one complement the other two, and vice versa? Are they equal and balanced or is one lesser than the other two? Think of these big three as an equilateral triangle laying flat and carefully placed on a center post; does it balance? As Mr. Miyagi from *Karate Kid* would say, "Sometimes what heart know, head forget." This is where you need to get out of your headspace and truly listen to your heart.

Is sex and/or intimacy one of your Three Pillars? It's important to insert this here because this is a common item that all genders will relate to and will likely appear on most people's Three Pillars. This is just as true for singles (even if in a period of abstinence) as it is for decades-long married couples and every person and situation in between. Sex is easy. That's what makes it so complicated. The basic act of sex is one of those things where when you're getting it you don't think about it; when you're not getting it, it's all you think about. Again, this is true for all genders. Granted, there are varying degrees of what satisfies an individual sexually—and even in committed relationships it can vary. It doesn't mean it's broken; it just means that it's a continual work in progress.

The act of sex comes very easy in some relationships and quite the opposite in others. Some relationships start out very sexually active and satisfying and stay that way for years, then diminish later for many reasons: age, hormone diminishment, childbearing, pain, cheating, low self-esteem, body composition, illness, loss of interest, and countless more reasons. The act of sex itself simply isn't the lowest common denominator if it's one of your Three Pillars, so let's work on it some more.

The act of sex itself feels great. Giving your body to another, receiving, pleasuring, being creative, talking, playing, slow and deep sometimes, and other times athletic and mind-numbing! It's awesome, but it's not a core value. It's not one of your Three Pillars. It's an extremely carnal instinct. But what separates you from a simple animal that just does it for procreation? Are you thinking that it's love that makes us different? That's a good start, but dig deeper still. All animals are sexual, but what makes us different? Yes, it's love, but you love your Uncle Dan. That doesn't mean you want to mate with him, right? What is it?

Think of a person in your life that knows you on the deepest levels—all your secrets, all your wrongs, all your faults, and all the things that make you tick. Who's that person in your life that if you asked them to tell you what they thought your Three Pillars are they could name them, or at least come really close. What is your relationship with that person? Did you develop that relationship with that person right when you first met them or did it develop over time? What is the magic between the two of you that will never diminish even if you didn't see each other for years and lived worlds apart? Is it intimacy? Is it passion? Is it compatibility? Is it friendship?

Ms. Jessie's Girl

I'll never forget the first time I met her in person. She was funny, sassy, and oh, she was so much fun to look at. Her personality was glowing with positivity and zeal for life. She was caring, playful, and she lit up the room wherever she went. She was the type of girl that other women either liked or hated. I titled her "Ms. Jessie's Girl," because I like the song lyrics, "Where can I find a woman like that—" except in real life I actually did.

The chemistry between us was undeniable from the first moment, and behind closed doors it was effortless and flowed like a raging waterfall. When we made love, it was literally like the world stopped spinning and even God himself would look down and wonder at his perfect creation. We didn't get to see each other as often as we would have liked, but we were extremely happy and content with our relationship. We would spend hours every day just texting, quick phone calls, telling stories about our childhood, and even past relationships. I want you to imagine Jenny and Forrest Gump: "We were like peas and carrots" all the time. When people saw us together, they immediately knew we were madly in love. To say we were compatible in every way was an understatement. We were best friends for life!

Friendship is the ultimate aphrodisiac in any intimate relationship in any language, any corner of the globe, and in any walk of life. True friendship has the power to overcome any obstacle, any challenge, and will be the hand in your hand through all time. When you have friendship as one of the Three Pillars, it will open the doors to an amazing, intimate sex life that will stay in your relationship even after the act of sex diminishes and for whatever reason. It takes work; it takes understanding; it takes forgiveness; it takes tons of communication; and above all else, it takes time. There isn't a formula for how friendship works versus its happy by-product (sex), but I loftly estimate that it takes a hundred hours of communication for even one hour of what you imagine to be your perfect sexual experience. The more communication and bonding you have outside the bedroom will come back tenfold in the bedroom.

The other two items on your Three Pillars list are just as important, and only you can decide what they are for you, but I do want to give you some pointers to consider. A huge one is your religion (if you have one); and if you don't, then that's a biggie too. I once had this newly married couple that I showed homes to for weeks before they found the perfect match for them. He was a doctor in his residency, and she was in IT. They were so cute together. She was the girl-next-door, blonde with great body shape and definitely came from the "right" family. He was from Pakistan but spent most of his childhood in the United States. He, too, came from the "right" family. She was steeped in Catholicism, and he was Muslim. On the surface they were the perfect couple. You could tell they were the happiest married couple ever—touching, laughing, flirting, had very similar interests, and their intelligence levels were on par with each other. They were very much on the same page with the location and type of home they wanted to purchase. Like I said, I spent countless hours with this couple over several weeks. When you spend that much time with a couple—and particularly in my line of work—you really get to see how a couple works together in multiple facets. I remember several instances where they asked me if they could view the home we were in just by themselves so they could explore and talk in private. I, of course, obliged. You're an adult, right? You can read between the lines. The more time I spent with them the more I could see that while they had come to some compromises regarding their vastly different religious perspectives, I could also sense an underlying angst in the relationship. They weren't blind to the fact that their future was going to be filled with challenges regarding coming from two religious viewpoints and family cultures. Here's the point regarding religion—as it ranks right up there with sex: Even if you do come from the same faith, you're going to have enough normal life-long challenges anyway. Then to add on top of that different beliefs regarding your faith is, in this writer's opinion, a formula for way-above-normal problems and painful challenges that can lead to resentments. At some point, someone in the relationship isn't going to be able to compromise. Danger Will Robinson, Danger! Now, I'm in no way touting one faith or way of believing above any other. I'm simply saying that if finding someone you're compatible with is a primary goal on this journey to bury your undateable nature, then seeking someone with similar beliefs is a wise choice.

Okay, so you've got your Three Pillars. You're set!

CHAPTER 4

The Three Bonuses

Now let's talk about the "Three Bonuses." These are three things that mean a lot to you. The way to think about these things is to think of your interests and the things you like to do. These aren't core values, but rather things that you enjoy about your life as a single person and that you hope to find in someone who shares these commonalities with you—even if it's just one of the three. For example, if you play in a band, sing, love music—and it's very much a part of your life—then seeking someone that shares that interest would be awesome. It doesn't mean that they play in a band like you do, but perhaps they played a musical instrument growing up and they understand how to read music. And when it comes to buying that super-expensive piano you've always wanted, you won't have to hard-sell them on the idea. See what I mean? Here's another example: Suppose you're a total health nut and you like to eat healthy and work out at least four times a week—and you've been doing it for years—the person you're seeking should share that passion with you so that when you make a leafy spinach salad at nearly every meal, they're not saying, "No, thanks" as they reach for a bag of their favorite chips. Plus, if you end up having kids or blending families, you don't have parental disputes regarding how the kids are going to eat. It's important to keep in mind that these special interests will increase and decrease at different times in your life, but your Three Bonuses are fundamentally a long-term part of your past, present, and future life.

If you're struggling to think about what these three things are because you're the type of person that just doesn't really have any special interests and your perfect Saturday is to sleep in late and hang around your house in your pajamas all day, well then, put that down. Keep in mind these things don't necessarily have to be an activity or a hobby; they can just be something that defines how you often spend your time. If you spend one day a month at Grandma's house, then that could be one of your three bonus items. If you read a book for thirty minutes every night before bed, then that counts. Maybe you're a hardcore superhero-movie person and even have the matching bed sheets, shoes, and undies to prove it; then that's a great one! These are simply life's little joys that bring you happiness, no matter how big or how small they are. The key is this: It's three things you've known about yourself for years, and it will always be a part of your life. Write down your three things.

1.

2.

3.

Got it? Great! If you were on a first date with someone and they brought up one of these Three Bonuses as something they are interested in, would your face light up like a Christmas tree? Would you get butterflies in your tummy and secretly be fist pumping the air and be like, "I want to have children with this woman!"? If that's how you feel then you've nailed the exercise. If your feeling is "Meh," then erase and—please, for the love of God—try again, because this is way too important to get wrong. Remember, dating is an investment of time in yourself and in another person. If you can't share one or more common interests that you've both had for years, then can you really expect a return on your investment? Probably not. What we're doing here is increasing your odds of finding a compatible match. When that happens, you'll learn that all this time you thought you were undateable was not only incorrect, it was nothing more than a strategic mistake; that is, you just didn't know "how" to date.

It's time for the big show! Date Night! The "first" date. Game time. Whoop Whoop! Time to showcase your Three Pillars and whip out your Three Bonuses like Dwayne Johnson carrying six little puppies in his big arms walking through downtown Manhattan. Ok, hold on now. Don't kick in the first-date dating-doors and walk in with guns blazing just yet. Yes, you're ready to talk, but the question is how do you bring it up? "Like, seriously, Bobby. You've given me so much confidence now, but what do I do when I'm actually sitting there staring at my date and I just want to vomit this stuff out?" In this section I could probably insert another whole book that deals with specific quips, quotes, date suggestions, and conversation starters. And I gotta tell ya, I'd probably love writing that book even more than this one, so stay tuned.

Now, back to the business of how you communicate about your Three Pillars and your Three Bonuses during the date, and some advice on the approach. Step one, you've met up and taken your seat wherever you're meeting. The location of the date isn't as important as your dating curb appeal and just being ready for an hour or two of lively conversation. There really isn't any rule about where to go on a first date: a small-venue concert, the park, a restaurant, etc. It's all good. However, I would avoid bringing your first date to the family reunion or Thanksgiving dinner! You need to meet in a location where you can be your true self and not be dealing with any outside forces or pressures.

Once you're seated and the conversation is ready to begin, I highly recommend starting the conversation like this: "I'm so excited to finally meet you. Tell me a bit about yourself." This does a couple of things. First, you're communicating that you're present and enthusiastic to be on the date. Second, it allows the person to talk about something with regard to themselves other than what they do for a living. Everyone talks about what they do for a living, and if that's their first response, that's totally okay. Listen intently, and let them answer completely. Then ask again like this: "That's awesome! Your job sounds really cool. So tell me about what makes you *you* and what you are passionate about." When the person you're with hears you ask the question this way, it might stop them in their tracks. Why? Because, frankly, this is a real question, and it's not what people are used to being asked. It hits below the surface and really challenges the person to think of a response that they've not "pre-scripted" and already answered for other people their entire career. As you're listening intently, you'll also be thinking about whether this "thing" they're answering with is compatible with one of your Three Pillars or

Bonuses that you also see as a core value or something you also enjoy doing. I promise, some delightful and fun dialogue will ensue. You don't need to go out of your way to try and relate or agree with everything they say. Just be yourself and be authentic. This conversation starter should help both of you easily transition into your other two topics and gives the other person the opportunity to listen to you as well. Remember this: People like to ask questions that they themselves would be happy to answer. Listen to those queues and allow the conversation to flow naturally and easily. This is a first date; you don't have to solve all the world's problems out of the gate.

Don't force it; just wait for it. I call this, "listening to the popcorn." What I mean is, when you put popcorn in the microwave and set the timer, rarely do you let the popcorn go the entire time of the timer.

Next—and when the moment is right—perhaps you can ask or share one of your Three Pillars. Don't force it; just wait for it. I call this, "listening to the popcorn." What I mean is, when you put popcorn in the microwave and set the timer, rarely do you let the popcorn go the entire time of the timer. Instead, you stand there and listen for just the right time for that last kernel to pop. Then you know it's time to take the bag out. Listen for it; that moment will come. If it doesn't, then no biggie. There's always date number two if you choose.

CHAPTER 5

Dating Curb Appeal

I've been a residential real estate agent for over fifteen years, and what I can tell you is that the term "curb appeal" is absolutely critical to any home sale. I simply don't care how spectacular the inside of the home is with its gleaming hand-scraped hardwood floors, master bath with pillars over the jacuzzi tub, and even the gourmet kitchen with commercial fridge and two ovens. Simply put, like a home, your curb appeal has got to be on point or you're better off not even showing up. We're going to officially dub this "dating curb appeal." By that I mean, I want you to imagine that you're meeting your date in front of the restaurant, at the curb. Get it? The stage is set. It doesn't matter how you met him/her, how long you've known each other, and how many pictures you've exchanged over Snapchat. First impressions are critical, and before any words are spoken he/she is going to see you walking up—your curb appeal has got to be on point. In short, you better knock his/her socks off. Otherwise, whatever you have to say during the date about your Three Pillars simply won't matter because in his mind he's standing at the curb looking at you walking up and wondering why he wasn't worthy enough for you to give him your best. Sorry, ladies, it's just a fact.

Men, the same is massively and equally true for you. Just because you're a dude and your first date is at a sports bar to watch a UFC fight doesn't mean you get to wear your favorite T-shirt just because it's got your favorite beer logo on it, a backwards ball cap and have gone unshaven for days. Listen, men, that's Saturday morning workout attire and only after you've been dating for several weeks. It's certainly not the right first-date curb appeal. Don't mess this up, ladies and gents. Don't do it. If "your style" is to dress down for everything in your life, well then, first-date night isn't that night. I'm not saying you gotta dress like it's Easter Sunday, but you gotta put some effort into it. Ladies, that means hair, nails, makeup, and at least—please—show at least 30 percent of your skin, not including the neck and face. And if you're self-conscious about your body composition, then I want to give you a tip about men and our psyche. For every 10 percent of your skin that you show us, the more we appreciate what we see. So if you're a big ole juicy girl, take my word for it, show more, not less. Yes, more! It doesn't mean dress slutty; it just means dress sexy! Dress like you meant to be on this special date and not that you simply showed up after the kids' soccer practice.

Bros, seriously, shave your face, use teeth whiteners, fix your hair, and have clean lines from your shoes to the top of your head. Women love symmetry and proportion. And for goodness' sake, get it through your head that the first date is about her and not you, so keep your pants zipped up and be prepared to listen way more than you talk.

Ms. Snaggletooth

So I got on a dating app, and boy, was that an experience! I was scrolling through that week's selection of potential first-date opportunities, and bam, there she was! She had five pictures—one of them in a swimsuit—and she had that kinda body that just made me dizzy: short, sporty, a perky B-cup, long hair, and oh, those bright red lips! We chatted, and hit it off right away. We met at a hip bar/restaurant in a "boujee" part of St. Louis called "The Hill," which is well known for its Italian heritage, population, and nightlife, and is a hot spot for dating in the metro. I was standing at the bar having a drink, the door opened to the front of the building, and there she was: all four feet, eleven inches in a short, little skirt, perfect hips, and a tight top that left her shoulders completely exposed. I'm sure she was wearing the most expensive push-up bra that Victoria Secret made; and let me tell ya, it was working! Hair was curled, red lips were on, makeup was on point, and even her earrings were in sync with her ensemble.

The front door was fifteen feet to where I was standing at the bar. And you know that scene in old movies where the jukebox screeches when someone walks in the door and everyone in the joint turns and looks at who just breezed in? Well, that was her. Like, I actually watched the entire bar turn and look at her, every step she made, right up to where I was now standing. "Sweet heaven on earth. I'm going to marry this girl tonight!" I actually watched one gal on my right literally scoff at her husband and slug him in the arm as he was staring just a bit too eagerly as this little jawbreaker walked up to the bar to greet me. "Yes! Yes! Yes! Thank you, Lord! Thank you sooooo much!" I actually bent down, put my arm around her waist and kissed her on her cheek (dangerously close to her right ear), and then whispered "WOW!" Listen, y'all, I can't make this stuff up; I'm not that imaginative. But I will say that I am often fortunate enough to see and pay attention to details that most don't see. Ok, so now for the funny part: As I engaged her in conversation I quickly noticed that she didn't turn to face me for any intimate eye contact whatsoever. I thought maybe she was super nervous so I ordered us a drink and just continued to face her, eagerly engaging in fun conversation. This went on for some time. She would not face me at all. What's the deal; did she have a bad zit or maybe horrible halitosis? This gal wasn't what she portrayed, and it did not take long to figure it out. She had extremely funky teeth—and I don't mean like bad genetics and "Oh, that poor thing." I mean, like a drug-infested meth mouth. I could quickly tell during the conversation that we were not the least bit compatible intellectually. And, she had the most obnoxious laugh I've ever heard. She sounded like Donkey in the movie *Shrek* when she laughed. You've heard Eddie Murphy laugh, right? That was her laugh! I ushered us both through the date quickly so that I could get this over with. Toward the end, she told me that she was "dropped off," didn't have a car, and "I'm okay, I'll just walk home." Which, of course, pulled on my heartstrings because I'm such a sappy guy. Seriously, though, I was thinking that she was probably going to offer me sex for money so she could get her fix. I offered to take her home and instead dropped her off at a Steak'n Shake which, according to her, was close enough to where she lived.

There are so many lessons I learned that night. Haha! Please laugh along with me. And here's the point: Other than her funky meth mouth, her dating curb appeal was a home run. Now, I know what you ladies are thinking: *Of course it was on point, because she was a drug whore.* And you know what? You very well could be right. Be careful and wary of those dating apps and profiles. There's some, shall we say, interesting things going on out there. But the point is this: Her pictures on the dating app were on point, and her curb appeal on the first date was on point. I could have left all the other stuff about her teeth out of the story and you'd be none the wiser. But I'm all about telling the truth. I'm also providing a couple of other ancillary points, which are: Dating apps are the equivalent of a resume, and their purpose is to get the interview. Second, people are often stone-cold liars and misrepresent who they are and what their intentions are. And it's not just men; it's women too. Can I get an amen?

For you guys and gals that are a bit more conservative with your dress, that's 100 percent ok. Was it tantalizing that this young "Trixie" showed up dressed with less than the 33 percent skin-showing standard that I enjoy? Yes, absolutely. But if she had shown up with only 20 percent, had a killer personality, made me laugh, and I could sense she was genuine friendship and dating material, then it definitely would have gone to a second date.

> *I had a track coach in junior high school that used to say, "How you 'start' the race is how you'll 'finish' the race," and dating is no different. Start your date ready to showcase how great you look and how dateable you are, regardless of what you think you look like.*

Dating curb appeal is a real thing, my friends. You better believe in it. I had a track coach in junior high school that used to say, "How you 'start' the race is how you'll 'finish' the race," and dating is no different. Start your date ready to showcase how great you look and how dateable you are, regardless of what you *think* you look like. You may think you're undateable, but trust me, you're not. Too tall, too short, too skinny, too fat, whatever. Show up with your best dating curb appeal; and even if it doesn't lead to more dates, you'll have a positive experience because you did your part, and you should feel good about yourself.

Ms. Bikini Model

I got this friend request on social media from a gal that lived several hours away. I scrolled through her profile to see what she was all about. She was a single mom, business owner, and a bikini model. She had several selfies, pictures with her kids, and was always smiling in her pictures. Given the name I gave her, it goes without saying she was drop-dead gorgeous. Understatement! We chatted on social media for a couple of weeks off and on, and it was a lot of fun. She had a super positive attitude and was funny as hell. Half the time I felt like I was chatting it up with a dude! Eventually, we exchanged phone numbers and didn't make any solid plans to meet up but simply left it as it would be great to meet up someday.

Someday came! She had family that lived on the other side of St. Louis, and she was coming for a visit soon. She wanted to know if I'd like to go out with her. My toes curled with excitement! She went to visit her family, left her kids there, and met up with me at my house. That part is a bit unorthodox, but given that she was from out of town and we'd really bonded via texting and video calls over several weeks, it was totally fine. I wasn't worried that she was an ax murderer or anything.

She pulled into my driveway, and like a golden retriever, I practically jumped out of the front door to greet her. She came inside, and we chatted and laughed for quite a bit. I let her use my bathroom to change clothes and get ready. She came into the kitchen and was wearing a skintight black cocktail dress with heels, curled hair, smoky eyes and, of course—my all-time fave— bright red lipstick. I'm sure the look on my face was priceless! We drank some wine and hit the road.

I took her to a restaurant I thought she'd like, and we spent hours just talking about anything and everything. Yes, there was some smooching! We knew there couldn't be any long-term dating due to the long distance, kids, sports, work, life—and in some ways that made the date easier because we both kinda knew we just had this one date to make all the magic happen.

During our conversation at the restaurant, we talked about our health and how important that was to both of us. We then, of course, proceeded to eat the most unhealthy things on the menu and drinking a fair amount of wine. Hey, it was date night, and we both worked hard at our health. This was a night to reward and celebrate that. We talked about parenting, our families, and things we both considered core values. At the time it occurred, it was the greatest date I'd ever experienced in my adult life! It's sad that we were so compatible but couldn't engage in anything long term; yet I was so grateful to have met someone that helped me realize I wasn't undateable after all!

A final word on this chapter: Above all else, be authentic and truthful with yourself, because there's nothing worse than going on a date, then another, and another where you're not being your true self—only to later morph into something that the other person doesn't even recognize based upon your first meeting. Ladies, if you're not a hair, nails, and makeup kinda gal, that's totally fine; just be yourself. Men, if you're only on the date because you're trying to get laid that week, then you're not being authentic in the dating process. What you'll find happens is that you'll be unsuccessful at having a meaningful relationship with someone that ultimately will lead to the type of intimacy you're wanting to have, and you'll be a hamster on a wheel going nowhere.

CHAPTER 6

Dating Etiquette

I suppose any book written on this topic would not be complete without some general pointers on what is considered good etiquette during a date. There is no differentiation in dating etiquette between the sexes. If you classify yourself as a human that is dating, then these dating etiquette points are for you. There is so much attention and polarization these days about genders—and I don't just mean males versus females—I mean all genders that are present on the dating battlefield today. This book is not written for any "one" gender; it's for anyone that is dating, not dating but would like to, and even for those in committed relationships.

Rule #1: Eye Contact. In my humble opinion, I believe that nothing says you are giving your date your full attention more than direct and intentional eye contact. Admittedly, this is difficult for some people because of their personality type, cultural upbringing, and a host of other reasons. Regardless, when you make eye contact with someone, it communicates that you're present in the conversation and you're actually attentive to what's going on during the date. Eye contact is so powerful because your eyes can communicate in ways that your words cannot; and at the same time, they can add more credit and value to your spoken words. Your eyes can flirt, they can express hurt, excitement, boredom, and every possible human emotion. But keep this in mind too: Some people can be very stoic in nature, and their eye contact can appear to be dry and unemotional. That's okay. The differences between all of us humans is what makes us unique. Plus, chances are that even the most stoic person, when ready, can offer massive eye-contact communication at the times it matters most. We've all heard that the eyes are the gateway to the soul, and I couldn't agree more. There are so many beautiful things about the human body, yet the eyes offer the richest colors of blue, brown, green, hazel, and more. They are gorgeous. They are works of art painted by the divine. Eye contact during dating is essential! If you're not an eye contact communicator, then this is a skill to work on—not only for dating, but for all of life's endeavors.

Rule #2: Be Yourself. This has a couple of meanings. First, it means that when you show up for the date you should be what you've represented to be. In this age of dating apps, the term "catfishing" is wildly true. For those that aren't familiar with this term, "catfishing" means that you overuse or abuse camera angles or filters to create an image of yourself that isn't true to life for what you actually look like on a daily basis. Don't be a catfish. It doesn't work no matter how many drinks your date has. Next, and more importantly, when you show up for a date, be your true self. Modifying your behavior for a date doesn't paint a true picture of your personality and whether you make it to a second or third date, or more. Eventually, your modified behavior will dissipate like vapor and your true colors will come out.

Rule #3: Be Kind. This is a popular term today. It's printed on T-shirts, shows up constantly on social media memes, and some companies have even adopted it as part of their culture. Being kind to someone doesn't mean kissing their ass or fake laughing at a less-than-funny joke. Hopefully, explaining what being kind to someone means isn't a topic that needs a lot of focus. The phrase stands by itself and is self-explanatory. But just in case it does need explanation, being kind simply means that you treat the other person with respect, value their opinions (even if you don't share the same), and use words, gestures, and actions that aren't off-putting to your date. Dating is like interviewing for a job: Show up with goodness and positivity in your heart and in your words.

> *Being dateable means that your words and gestures communicate to the other person that you're a well-adjusted, available, and smart person with a mature emotional IQ who values not only your own time but their time as well.*

Rule #4: Be Dateable. Being dateable means that your words and gestures communicate to the other person that you're a well-adjusted, available, and smart person with a mature emotional IQ who values not only your own time but their time as well. One more thing: The term "ghosting" is a popular term these days. It's when one person stops communicating abruptly, leaving the other person completely wondering what the heck happened. Ghosting is a big no-no and will hurt your reputation as a dating person, and social media will make that all too easy.

Rule #5: Be On Time. If your date is set for a certain time and place, then it's common courtesy to be on time. Being fashionably late so you can make a grand entrance isn't a cool thing to do. Being on time says a lot about what type of person you are and how you approach many aspects of your life. I have a famous saying that I've used for years with my various sales teams: "When you're early you're on time, when you're on time you're late, and when you're late you're rude."

Rule #6: Pay the Bill. This is a sticky topic, but to be honest, it doesn't have to be. A good rule of thumb is if you invited the other person out for the date, then you should pay. I'm an old-fashioned sorta guy, so I always pick up the tab. But the longer I am single and dating, I've learned that if the gal wants to pay, then it's okay, especially if she asked you out. However, you should never go on a date unless you're financially prepared to pay your half—or even the whole thing. It's just a good idea in case the unexpected happens. That will rarely happen, but it's best to be prepared.

Rule #7: Easy on the Alcohol/THC. Having a drink during your date is totally acceptable and normal. But having three before you leave your house so that you can "warm up" and settle yourself isn't a good idea. The same is true during the date. Alcohol and other substances like THC that lower your inhibitions can lead you to not be your authentic self, and you'll end up regretting something you said or how you acted. The same is true for stimulants such as too much coffee, or even cocaine. If you're a daily user of substances that are known for altering behavior, then you need help and you should halt all dating activities.

Rule #8: Don't Interrogate. Previously, I mentioned that dating is like interviewing for a job. Asking fun questions and passing the ball back and forth in the conversation is totally the right thing to do, but interrogating your date is poor sportsmanship in the dating game. Your goal is to see if this person is worth your time and if you're worth theirs. It's not to find out every piece of information about that person in a one-to-two-hour date. Remember: This is a date, not a boardroom meeting. It is certainly not a full-out interrogation with your date metaphorically handcuffed to the little bar across the table while you beat them with questions and blow your cigarette smoke in their face.

Rule #9: Don't Dominate the Conversation. You've probably noticed that in most relationships there is typically one person that's a bit more chatty than the other. That's perfectly normal. But when you're dating someone new, keep your gun in the holster and treat the conversation like a good ole tennis match. You hit the ball, he/she hits back, and so on and so forth. You don't have to treat it like speed dating where each person gets their time to talk and then it's your turn. But if you sense that you've just talked nonstop for more than a couple of minutes, then it's courteous to pass the baton. In my experience when this rule isn't observed, what often happens is one person has the best date ever while the other feels like it was one of the worst. Sharing is caring. Share the conversational space as equally as possible. If you're a carefree extrovert and he's a stoic introvert, then it's easy to just keep talking to fill the air. In that case, it's totally fine for there to be air in the conversation. As an extrovert myself who is naturally attracted to introverts, I just have to remind myself to initiate questions to help the other person start (and continue) talking. Folks, this is an art, not a science. Trial and error is to be expected.

Rule #10: Limit Talk About Past Relationships. Whether it's your first date or your fifth, at some point talking about past relationships most certainly will be a topic. Yes, it's ok to say it's not a topic you're interested in, but it's better to already know what you want to say. It's also best to keep it light and don't talk negatively about the other person, because it will paint the wrong picture of you. If your past guy or gal was a drunk, abusive, a cheater, or anything worse, it's best to just share the highlights of the relationship in a positive light and what life lesson you learned, and then move on. The same is also true if your past relationship was wonderful and it's totally a mystery to you why it ended. The last thing you want is for the new guy/gal wondering if you're still in love with the last relationship and, if so, how could they possibly measure up?

Ms. Super-Hot Stuff

It was ninety-five degrees! It was a Saturday afternoon, and besides the heat, the humidity in Missouri was sweltering to the point that you could carry a towel in your hip pocket to wipe your brow even while standing in the shade. I was meeting this gal at one of my favorite places that offered a super cool outdoor patio with lots of fans, umbrellas, spray misters, and live music. Billy G's restaurant is like being at your favorite beachside cabana bar and grill. It's well known in Kirkwood, MO, as being the "Who's Who" of dating and networking and offers great aristocratic-people watching. We had arranged the date days before, and I even said to her, "Hey, it's gonna be hot; are you sure this is okay with you? If not, we can meet indoors somewhere." Her response was, "Yeah, for sure. Sounds perfect." I was literally standing on the curb waiting for her. I was wearing my favorite fashion-forward sneakers, khaki shorts, and a tight athletic-cut, black v-neck T-shirt. I have an athletic build, so that's me being "on point" for a date when it's hotter than hell out. I had a fresh haircut from just that morning, my teeth were extra white, and I was, well, ready to meet this fresh face, summer hottie and listen my guts out! Ya know, I have great dating etiquette; and every guy knows to let the girl do most of the talking on the first date!

I saw this gal walking toward me. She looked at me, then put her head down. I turned my head away, then back toward her again. She was now about thirty feet away from me. I kinda did this eye-squint thing because I couldn't tell if this was someone I had met before or if it was my date. Sure enough, this was my date! I was shocked. I was so shocked that it actually showed on my face. And I know that because she asked me, "Are you okay?" For which I responded, "Yup. Ready to go in?" She was wearing closed-toe flats, full-length jeans, a T-shirt undershirt, and a heavy long sleeve cover that was buttoned nearly to the top. She had no makeup on, and her hair was totally bedhead. You know that emoji that you text to people, the one with the image of the little guy that's flat-hand smacking his own face? Yeah, insert that here. It's squelching hot out, and this gal is dressed as if she was going to a rural family reunion on Thanksgiving morning after she's been cooking all day and didn't sleep a wink the night before. Even though she was covered up more than a nun, I could still tell that she had a HWP (height and weight proportionate) body and an overall average figure, which is totally fine by me. Sure, she had a little mom-bod action going on, but that stuff doesn't bother me as long as the overall symmetry is aesthetically pleasing and a gal puts at least a C-plus effort into her makeup and hair. Yes, I said, "C-plus," not "A-minus," which means I'm pretty down to earth and realistic, especially in this heat. I love a smoking hot supermodel kind of look, but I also very much like the girl-next-door vibe just as much and, most of the time, probably more. Rant over. On with the date details!

We took our seats, and surprise, surprise—because the place was already packed—we got a table toward the front of the restaurant which had no shade, no fans, and the tables with umbrellas were all taken. And, given the high noon time of day, the sun was beating down on us like we were in the Mojave Desert. Quickly—oh so quickly—I could tell this young lady had major self-esteem issues. Mega! Huge! "Ugh, not again," I thought to myself as I watched her sweating to death. Ok, so at this point I'm switching into big-brother mode because I know right away this date wasn't going to have any really flirty or intellectual conversation. Instead, it turned into a conversation all about her past relationship(s) and what a dating Holocaust survivor she was and how she's barely hanging on by a thread as a single mom. Her past dating stories were an identical match to her fall floral overshirt in the middle of summer—a total disaster! I could go on and on about this specific date and countless others like it I've experienced.

A little foreshadowing here, my Undateable friends: We're going to have a whole chapter just talking about resentment and past-failed relationships, so stay tuned.

I listened and drank as much as I could before the sun melted it out of me and the date was concluded. We walked out of the restaurant, and I could tell she was staying close to my side because she really wanted to kiss me. Why, I have no idea, because that was the worst date ever. When we got just outside the door, I thanked her for her time, gave her a firm hand squeeze and started to walk across the street toward the parking lot. I could see out of my periphery that she was just standing there dumbfounded. She even called out, "So that's it?" For which I responded with—well, nevermind, I didn't respond. I just kept walking and played like I didn't hear her. I know, I know, ladies, you hate me again. Listen, I never said I was Mr. Perfect in every situation. And even as I'm writing this book, I'm still learning from my past experiences and dating mistakes. However, this is only the beginning of this story. The next part is where it gets really good and totally proves my point about how important dating etiquette and curb appeal are.

Several days went by—and trust me, there was absolutely no reason for either of us to reach out to the other. The message was clear that that date was our first and our last. But she did reach out to me via text inviting me for a second date. We text chatted a bit, and finally I wrote her back saying, "I'm thinking a lot about our 'meeting' the other day. I definitely enjoyed it! Thank you; and, yes, I would do it again. And, I don't foresee a romantic future from my end. I hope it's okay to just speak with truth and compassion 'cause I don't see two people like us having any time to waste in pursuit of the wrong thing or misleadings whatsoever." In other words, I did what singles affectionately refer to as "putting someone in the friend zone." Her response was, "It was my big feet, wasn't it? I applaud the honesty and appreciate that more than anything. If you ever want another 'meeting' of the minds, reach out." There was some other idle chitchat, and finally she wrote, "Any constructive truths about me you'd like to throw at me? I'm not full of confidence and really not sure what I'm doing. I'm still a work in progress." So I thought to myself for a moment, "Maybe I can really help this gal out and genuinely help her get on a better path for dating. It's not my place, and maybe it would be better to just avoid this additional contact altogether," but I simply couldn't help myself. I'm a super positive and compassionate person, and I love to inspire people to be their best no matter what it is.

I offered to have a Facetime call with her later that week. We would talk, and I'd just be honest with her about my thoughts regarding the date. She accepted my invitation. A couple of days later we met via video chat, and the conversation commenced. She was sitting on her back patio, and I was in my home office. We were both having a glass of wine, and the conversation began something like this: "You're a beautiful, young woman," (blah, blah, blah) "and I could tell you were dealing with low self-esteem. That was very apparent during our first date."

As the conversation unfolded, I was very gentle and slow because I genuinely wanted to help her and not reinforce her already-low self-esteem mindset. We spoke for a couple of hours at least, and it was awesome! I was super honest with her about how she was dressed and how she went on and on about her past horrific relationship experiences and how that is what ultimately led to her mindset about not having self-worth and low confidence.

She listened intently, and there were a lot of tears. But we also shared laughs and more stories on both our parts. Honestly, this experience with her was actually a great date, even though it wasn't a date at all. It was more akin to one friend telling another friend, "Look, Girl, we gotta talk about your situation, and you need to get your life together." She was extremely grateful for the information and the honesty, and we even kept in touch after that night.

A few weeks went by, and she sent me a text to let me know she had a first date that night. She took a selfie, and she was wearing a spaghetti-strap shirt, and her hair and makeup were amazing. Seriously, she was Ms. Super-Hot Stuff for her date—and I don't mean the summer heat! I complimented her profusely. Wow! Where was that girl on *my* date with her? Several weeks went by, and I saw a post of her on social media with her new boyfriend. He was very handsome and a total beefcake—athletically speaking. She was happily dating an absolutely awesome guy, and I could tell from her smile she was in a great place and very passionate about her newfound romance!

Dating etiquette is for real, y'all, and it takes more than just knowing; it takes practice. You don't have to be perfect, but the rewards of knowing these behaviors and tweaking the smallest things to rid yourself of your undateable nature and bad habits can make all the difference. The Golden Rule says, "Treat others as you want to be treated." Personally, I believe in the Platinum Rule: "Treat others as *they* want to be treated."

CHAPTER 7

Resentment is The Mothership of All Relationship Failures

It's impossible to go through life and not experience resentment toward failed relationships. You can read all the positive social media memes and engage in countless hours of therapy, and it won't completely eliminate your resentment toward the bad things that have happened to you or even your guilt about wrong-doings you've committed toward others. To "resent" is to be a normal human being. Thousands of psychologists would agree—and I would strongly argue—that resentment is a primary reason why so many of us have become undateable. What's the popular saying? "Life's a bitch," and then quickly followed by "Now get over it."

Getting over our past relationship resentments is tough. It gets even tougher the older you get. If you're in your twenties, never been married, don't have kids, then getting over past relationship resentments is way easier than if you're in your forties and were married for twenty years with kids and a very bitter divorce. It's even worse if you throw in a couple of marriages. But here's the deal: You can live your life staring in the rearview mirror or you can firmly press the gas and enjoy the big ole windshield with sunshine and many more miles of beautiful road to travel that lay ahead. I suggest the latter!

Resentment is the mothership of all past relationship failures. It's also the mothership of future relationship failures if you don't let that crap go!

The heart is a muscle; and the longer you hold on to that resentment, muscle memory sets in and it becomes harder and harder to let it go and make a change for the better. Your heart holds on to that resentment for so long that eventually it becomes your normal thinking and will spill over into every aspect of your life.

Remember in elementary school on the last day of school when you had "field day," where one class was pitted against another in a fierce game of tug-of-war? Remember that feeling you got in your gut as you gripped that thick hemp rope and held on for dear life and pulled your heart out? You could feel that rope burn on your palms the next day, right? Imagine that same feeling, except internally, and instead of a minute or two it can last years. That's years of wasted time! I'm not a purest when it comes to the concept of "forgive and forget," but the premise has merit. At some point, if you want to run your little romantic heart out toward second base, you have to take your foot off first base. You have to let go of that burning rope, because the longer you hold on to it, the harder it is to let go. The heart is a muscle; and the longer you hold on to that resentment, muscle memory sets in and it becomes harder and harder to let it go and make a change for the better. Your heart holds on to that resentment for so long that eventually it becomes your normal thinking and will spill over into every aspect of your life. When that guy broke your heart, or that gal cheated on you when she was out of town, or even when that stupid high school boyfriend broke up with you over something that today seems so ridiculous, that heart muscle has a memory, and the grip it has on your life affects everything.

I'm not a doctor, and I don't have a PhD in anything. Nor am I a licensed counselor. Regardless, I am qualified to say this. Just like you, I have a past, and the one thing that affects my current relationships more than anything is my reflection on past relationships. Forgiveness is noble. If you can get to that place, as I have, then it's absolutely the right headspace to be in, and I recommend it. But it's not the first step. Hell, I would argue that it's not even a necessary step. But what you do have to get to is a place where you have accepted what happened to you, take ownership—if any part of it was your fault—and ultimately learn from it. Look for those signs in the future, and for love's sake, let that baggage go and move on.

Ms. Baggage

Not all my dating experiences ended after the first date. Yes, I actually went on multiple dates with the same person from time to time. This particular gal worked for a well-known law firm and had been there for several years. She owned her home, was my kinda beautiful, had a big heart, came from a good family, athletic, and adventurous. I really have nothing negative to say about her whatsoever, other than one thing: Whenever we went out, and no matter where the conversation started, it always ended up with her talking about an ex-boyfriend—and not just the past one, but the last few. I really liked this girl. I was even falling for her. When the conversation got off track on yet another tangent about one of her exes, I sat and listened intently for the right time to steer it back toward talking about us or some other positive topic. Sometimes it worked; but many times, no matter how hard I tried, it eventually got back to the topic of her exes. Hell, it happened so systematically that at times I even found myself being the one to bring up the topic. I was getting sucked into the pattern. Ugh! It got to the point where I wanted to say to her, "Hey Babe, when we go out tonight, I want to ask if you'll make an effort not to talk about any of your exes." I never did, because once I got to the point of that type of thinking, I knew it was just time to throw in the towel, which I did. Plus, the things she was resentful for were actually pretty normal relationship challenges and nothing extreme, such as abuse, cheating, or any other horrific event. I wanted to gently grab her by the face with both hands and say, "Babe, these past issues you've had are normal; why are you still carrying this baggage?" I never did that either. Perhaps I should have.

Here's the thing: When you're dating that seemingly undateable person, keep in mind that we all have a myriad of past experiences and past resentments that we're carrying into our future, and you have to know what your level of tolerance is. Plus, that day will come where you'll be the one dredging up your past resentments. It's inevitable. It's normal. It's going to happen. The key here is to be working on your issues and preparing your undateable heart to be open to someone else's baggage, just like you hope they'll be open to yours.

This is also where dating someone who's at your emotional IQ level is important. If you've dealt with your resentments in a positive manner and you're dating someone that hasn't, then you can be part of their healing process. But keep this in mind: Do you want a girl- or boyfriend or do you want a project? Dating someone that's on par with your emotional IQ level is important because it's easier to stay connected equally rather than one person pulling while the other is holding back. I suppose an argument can be made that two people with a lot of resentment baggage can pull each other up, but at the same time, that's simply not realistic unless they both commit to the same "self-work" that it takes to get over past resentments—the type of work that typically is done solo and not with someone you're dating. That's what is commonly referred to as "trauma bonding," which is the equivalent of asking two drowning people to rescue each other.

We hear all the time about the importance of marriage counseling, but not counseling for couples who are dating. Marriage counseling, by and large, is for committed couples that are working on *their* issues more so than on issues before they were married. Not always, but most of the time. Plus, in cases where a married couple starts counseling as a couple, it's very common that at some point one of the two ends up doing one-on-one counseling to delve deeper into past resentments that have nothing to do with the marriage and/or prior to the marriage. If you're single, and you know in your heart you're dealing with resentment from past relationship entanglements, you're best served by seeking solo counseling rather than waiting until you're in a committed relationship. Why? Because history has a way of repeating itself. Deal with those resentments before it repeats itself again and again. Commit to the "self-work" it will take to let go of that burning rope before it renders you permanently undateable!

Ms. Insecure

I went on one date with this gal I had known for quite some time. There was always this chemistry between us, this awkward but fun heat! Like, when there's one piece of cake left, and it's just sitting on the counter; you walk by it all day, and finally you just can't take the pressure any longer and you shove that sugary chocolate goodness in your piehole and don't even bother getting a fork. You know the type I'm talking about. She had thick, luscious brown hair, Angelina Jolie lips, athletic build, and she was remarkably intelligent and successful. This was the type of girl you could tell was a bit quiet and reserved at first but that would later be—well, I'll just say it—a lioness in the bedroom. Her body language screamed, "Take me and do whatever you want; I'll let you! Release me from my boardroom boredom and enslave me like a bad, little kitty!" All of you know exactly the type I'm talking about.

We talked off and on for a long time, mostly via text, and it was always brief and never flirty. Mostly, it was like a life "check in" from time to time just to keep a pulse on things—about the same you'd do with your mom if she hasn't heard from you in a few weeks. Even at times when we were clearly not seeing anyone, neither of us asked, "Hey, would you like to meet up sometime for a drink?" Honestly, I always kinda felt like I needed to wait for her to tee that up. No specific reason why, just my gut instinct. I'm all too happy to pursue the right gal for a fun date night, but this particular fantastic gal just had to be handled differently than most. So I waited and waited. Finally, she initiated. We planned a little outdoor excursion. As the day got closer, it looked like it was going to rain. She messaged me and said she would understand if I wanted to reschedule. Honestly, I think she was very nervous and was perhaps looking for an "out," but because she asked *me* out she couldn't cancel. Perhaps she was hoping I would. There was no way in hell I was going to bow out. I genuinely wanted to spend time with her and get to know her. So, onward and upward.

The day of our date arrived, and we met up for our outdoor adventure. What we didn't expect to happen was the just-above-freezing rain. Finally, after a few hours of frolicking around, she said to me, "Hey, if you want to get out of the weather, we can go to my place." She quickly added, "We can sit on my patio by the fire." That was smart of her. Basically, that was code for, "Hey, I'm having fun and I want to continue, but you're not getting laid just 'cause we're going to my house." I thought to myself, "Haha! Roger that, Cutie. No problem!" We went to her house, opened a bottle of wine, and the date continued. We had great wine and great conversation. The more wine we drank, the more our outdoor adventure morphed into adventurous conversation. But not how you think—not yet anyway.

She began talking about her most recent long-term past relationship and how the guy had a small package and wanted to do weird things in the bedroom to seemingly "make up" for what he perceived as his inadequate manhood. She didn't even care about his package—I mean, she was in a very long-term relationship with the guy, so clearly she accepted that. It's not even why they broke up, not even close. Not even on her radar screen of reasons! So, men, take note of that!

This is where it got really interesting. During their relationship of many years, it became apparent that his low self-esteem and insecurities were being projected onto her, by him, and she bought into it. She started asking me questions about what men wanted, what men liked, and even asked me very personal questions about what I thought of her appearance and so, so much more. Look, this isn't a mom-porn book, so I'm going to limit how much I say here. I'll say just enough to convey my point.

Right there on her patio and in broad daylight on a cold and rainy day—and with no prompting from me whatsoever—she stood up, took her clothes off—rather quickly I might add—and let me look at her naked body with nothing more than a blanket draped over her shoulders. It all happened so quickly. And before I even knew what was happening, we were just in that moment. I studied the, shall we way, finer details of her entire body while she asked questions and I answered them. I wish I could say we were having a super hot, seductive moment, but to be honest, it was more, well, academic. She had serious questions, and she demanded honest answers. What can I say? I guess I was the lucky guy—or was I? Honestly, I'm still a bit confused by it all. All I can say is this: Her body was gorgeous, and I have absolutely no idea why she had any self-esteem issues with her body whatsoever. She not only had a gorgeous face and hair, but all of her was, frankly, pretty perfect! WOW!

I have two very important points to make about the afore-mentioned anecdote. First, your past relationship resentments are yours and yours alone to deal with. If you're depending on the next person to save you from your resentments, then you're going to be sadly disappointed. Second—and this is so important—the past resentments you're burdened with aren't 100 percent your fault; they're shared between you and that other person, or peo-ple. Chances are very good that they projected their own issues on you and you took ownership of them as if they were yours too. So what you can glean from this is that if you take your resent-ments into the next relationship, not only are you not dealing with your current and past resentments, you're adding other peo-ple's past resentments to your own list, exponential-relationships deep. Those past resentments do not belong to you; they are not yours to own or deal with. It's no wonder the divorce rate goes up in the second marriage and still higher in the third. Get it? We're all broken and have baggage in some way, and it's up to you to get over it however you go about doing that.

I can't say enough about the importance of investing time and money in an experienced, licensed counselor. Take all the time and money you need to get yourself whole again. I promise you from the bottom of my heart, it will be worth it. The process of "self-work" is the greatest investment you'll ever make. You've spent hundreds, if not thousands, of hours and money invest-ing in your career education—now do it for your heart and your mind. You wash your clothes. You wash your car. You wash your dishes. When something is dirty, it must be cleaned before it can be used again. Commit to the "self-work" you need to do. Wash your mind and cleanse your heart of your past resentments before you date and before you keep believing you're undateable. Being undateable is a current state of mind; it's not a long-term reality. Own it, treat it, heal it. And, my brothers and sisters, move the heck on to your better life, whether you remain single or find love ever after!

CHAPTER 8

Everyone in Your Universe is an Actor in Your Play—You're the STAR!

More than any other area in this book, in this chapter I want to go out on a limb. If you're a book critic, an educated philosopher, a relationship expert, or have a PhD, then this will be the chapter you'll love to critique and criticize more than any other—or at least I hope you will. Plus, this chapter will probably paint me as a borderline crazy person. So let's do this!

If you've seen the movie *The Matrix*, then you know that the main character, Neo, is torn between two worlds: the real world and the computer-generated Matrix world. That is a digital world that, in every sense appears real, even to the point that if you die while in the Matrix, your body in the real world will also perish. In the Matrix, what the mind perceives the body believes.

For those who haven't been fortunate enough to watch this spectacular Hollywood blockbuster, the name Neo is an anagram for "The One." His character is "the one" destined to save humanity from the false realities of the Matrix by conquering its architect. He uses spectacular hand-to-hand combat and spoon bending, superhero-type powers where he uses his mind's abilities to alter the reality of the Matrix. You, too, are "the one," and you are capable of designing your universe to behave exactly the way you "will" it to. You are the main character in your play, and I wish you to imagine that everyone else around you is simply an actor reacting to your willpower—and then challenging you to be better, faster, stronger, and more capable of anything you've ever imagined possible.

So what in Sam Hill does this have anything to do with being undateable? Take a deep breath and think about this: You perceive you are undateable not because of reality, but because you've created a false Matrix-type reality for yourself. You've made a construct of your emotions and your thoughts that prevents you from graduating to the next level. This construct isn't real; it's false. Mindset is everything, and your current mindset is stuck on believing that you can't reach the level of enlightenment in your dating and romantic ambitions. This construct has not only handicapped you from your destiny, it has crippled your relationship-development abilities in all aspects of your life. Imagine your body, your mind, your heart, and your soul as your dream car but with handicap license plates. You don't even know it, but you're actually putting on display for all the world to see that you're an undateable handicapped dater. Just because you get to park closer to the front entrance because of your handicap license plate, it doesn't make life any easier for you, and you know it.

Being undateable is mind over matter except in a negative way. Using your own mind and the environment around you,

you've convinced yourself that because of your handicap, the rest of the world must treat you differently, feel sorry for you. Tell you that you're right for how you feel. Tell you that you deserve better and that God will bring the right person when the time is right.

Right now, this very minute, you are surrounded by people that are enabling your behavior. You seek their counsel and their companionship because subconsciously you desire to stay in your weakened state. You have lived in your false construct for so long that you've forgotten it's not reality and is simply a purgatory of emotions and thoughts you are not actually meant for. You are not the main actor in your spectacular movie any longer; you're just another mindless robot like everyone else in the Matrix. Am I wrong?

In every great movie, there is a character that guides the main character to his/her victory. In the movie *The Matrix*, the infinite character of wisdom and prophecy is Morpheus. Morpheus doesn't rescue Neo from the false constructs of the Matrix but simply guides him to make a choice. He can take the red pill— and a very unpleasant truth will be revealed to him—or he can take the blue pill and remain in his false ignorance. Clearly Neo doesn't take the blue pill or it would have been a very short film that amounted to nothing. Neo, unsure of himself, unbelieving and afraid, chooses the red pill, and the real reality is revealed to him. It was ugly! He was awakened after a lifetime of living in the Matrix as just another mindless character living a life that went nowhere and was meaningless. I want to be your Morpheus. Take the red pill and go with me to defeat this false emotional construct you've created for yourself. You can be the most devout, religious person in history yet you are blessed and burdened with the simple truth that you are designed to be a free-thinking human being that has free will and the ability to choose your path. This ability to choose sets humans above all other living creatures on earth. You alone have the choice to get out of that wheelchair of your undateable, self-defeating attitude, retire your old thinking once and for all, and build new and healthy constructs in the form of human relationships, romance, and all forms of human interaction.

Here's a sample of what your new beginning looks like. How you date or don't date is a mirror of your current relationships. Have you ever heard the phrase, "You are the average of the people you hang out with the most?" Why do you think dating apps are a multibillion-dollar industry? Because some very smart people realized that many people can't break free from their current crippling patterns within their daily environments. Then they go online and create a new identity in hopes that they will attract love ever after using their new online identity. Wow, kinda sounds like another version of *The Matrix*, doesn't it? Digest that for a minute.

For those of you that have or are doing online dating, you just had your mind blown! Dating apps are a shortcut. They're the new middleman to making the undateable, dateable again. But, as is true with all things regarding the human condition, technology won't replace you. It won't go on the date for you anymore than it's going to help you design your new reality. Dating apps are attempting to be your Morpheus, that infinitely wise man that shows you the way to happiness. Total horse crap! Lies, lies, lies! It's not the app that's lying to you; it's you, my friend. The app is merely a door that opens and closes upon the tap of your finger on your mobile phone's lifeless glass screen. It's not the real you no matter how truthful you attempt to create your profile.

Whether you're using dating apps or more traditional means of finding your dating groove, you are well served to remember that you are the main character in your play, and you, my awesome friend, are the star. If your star is bright, then you'll be great at dating. Don't let anyone diminish your star. If you're a work in progress, then remember this: Every famous Hollywood actor started on smaller gigs and worked their ass off to climb their way to stardom—and there were no shortcuts!

———

Ms. Impossible

I grew up in a very poor county in the state of Missouri before I moved to the big city. It was primarily an agrarian area with most of the county's economy surviving on agriculture products, ranging from crops to cows and everything in between. It was poor for many reasons, but that's a whole other unrelated topic. Whenever you live in a poor area, alcoholism and other forms of addictions are pervasive and even bragged upon. "How many beers did you drink last night, Billy?" "Ahhhh, only a case. I got started late." In most people's high schools, you can remember that one girl or that one guy that was the "stinky" kid in your class. In my area, it was closer to half the kids rather than only just a few. Being pregnant in high school was more akin to a badge of honor than it was an embarrassment. It meant you had your life together and that you were ready for adulthood. High school was barely a necessity (outside of state law), and it was merely something you begrudgingly suffered through to get a diploma to make your parents happy.

I remember being in elementary school and taking the bus to school every day. We had one section of town that was particularly well known for being the welfare part of town. It had lots of really run-down houses, multiple cars parked in the yard and cluttered with lots of kids' outdoor toys, empty beer cans, and enough cigarette butts to start a paper mill. On one particular day, this little girl in my class got on the bus, and she was wearing no shoes. Yes, you heard me right; she got on the bus wearing only dirty, holey socks. Her family had a name around town for being late on bills, owing people money, always taking handouts from local churches, and were raging alcoholics. And you didn't dare cross one of them or you'd get your ass kicked. You see, when you grow up like that, in such a rural area, all you have is your pride and your badass attitude. My observation, understanding, and empathy for others started at a very young age—and especially for those people who were deemed "undesirables."

The bus driver saw that she wasn't wearing shoes, and he told her to sit in the front seat right behind him. I remember thinking to myself that maybe she was going to be in trouble. I was a kid and thought young-kid thoughts. What I realize now as an adult is that he wanted to save her from being teased and ridiculed by the older kids sitting in the back of the bus. Kids are cruel, and the farther you sat in the back of the bus the crueler you were. Your position on the bus was like a thirty-minute hierarchy that a kid had to survive every day going to school. Even the middle wasn't safe! I wasn't a stinky kid, but even I was bullied, so it is very relatable to me.

In my little town, all kids K-12 rode the bus together, not like a lot of metro areas today where there are multiple buses going to different schools: elementary, junior high, and high school. I gotta tell ya, a lot of bad stuff I learned about growing up happened right on the school bus. Like I said, she was in my class and the school was small, so it's not like I wasn't going to run into her later on during the day. During lunch, I saw the school nurse bring her to the cafeteria and put her in line with the rest of us. She was wearing beat-up boy's sneakers that were at least three sizes too big for her. I don't know what could have been worse for her, not wearing shoes at all or being told to wear the ones she was wearing.

Years went by, and eventually I moved to a different school in a different town. My bullying was so bad that my parents moved me to a different high school just to keep me out of fights. See, I wasn't kidding about my being bullied. After I graduated high school, more than a decade went by and my old school had a high school reunion. I was invited even though I didn't graduate from there. I was nervous about going, but I did have some friendships; and, of course, the whole point is to see who "made it" in the world and who didn't. I was sitting at a table at this old VFW hall, and in walked this show-stopping, jaw-dropping, stunning female. No one had a clue who she was. In my little town, people were very clicky in those days, especially if you didn't fit in. If you were an "undesirable," you were cast out. She just kinda stood there for a moment looking around. It was as if she was contemplating the decision she should have made before she walked in; that is, *am I going to actually do this?* She turned slowly and, with increasing speed, made her way confidently up to the bar. She placed her drink order and just stood there facing the bar. It was clear she was not going to turn around to face everyone that was nonchalantly looking at her. I swear she was going to catch on fire! I was a good forty feet away, and my heart was like a thermal scanner looking at her. I could feel everything she was feeling in that moment. So, me being me, I went up to her to break the ice because someone had to address the white elephant in the room—and God uniquely designed me to be just that guy. She turned around, and my jaw dropped! It was her. The one! This had to be impossible. How? I'm more known for my bluntness than I am for my smoothness or charm, and I'm sure it read all over my face at that moment. It wasn't long before people began to realize who she was, and a group of the "back then" popular girls came up to greet her as well. During our few minutes together, she briefly told me that she had made her way through college and was now living in the city and was doing excellent.

I swear she was going to catch on fire! I was a good forty feet away, and my heart was like a thermal scanner looking at her. I could feel everything she was feeling in that moment.

Ms. Impossible achieved the unachievable. She shattered the mold of her upbringing and made her own way. She swallowed that jagged little red pill and kicked her false reality in the face with lethal force. She became the star of her own play in the construct she alone built. She put in the work. She took the road less traveled and made a very successful and suitable life for herself. This is a story of a young woman who demolished all mental and emotional barriers and defied the greatest of odds that any one of us can have: a bad upbringing.

If you think you're undateable, think again. You are simply going to school each day barefoot on the handicap-enabled short bus; and as long as you choose to stay on it, you won't graduate to the next level. Are you ready to graduate? Are you done experimenting with the shortcuts to solve your undateable dilemma? Your answer better be "Yes"; and if you're not sure, then start at the top of this chapter and read it as many times as it takes!

To that little, malnourished, poor girl I knew in elementary school: I am so proud of you, and I am blessed to be one of the characters in your play. You are a bright and shining star, and you have my standing ovation!

CHAPTER 9

Swords & Shields

I personally struggle with this. If you're single, I'm sure you can relate. You meet someone and start dating. All seems well, then that inner voice starts coming out, that still, small voice that acts like the devil on your shoulder whispering in your ear about what's wrong with the person or the relationship. Hell, for some of us, it's not a whisper at all; it's a full-blown yelling voice in our head. The more often it speaks, the louder it gets. So when the going gets tough, do you make up or break up? That is the question.

Many of us present ourselves in dating by wielding either a sword or a shield. Despite how positive and optimistic a person I am in my day to day life, I'm a "shield" guy when it comes to relationships; that is, I'm on the defense. I didn't used to be, but my experiences brought me to this place. Many of you are all sword, meaning that you're full steam ahead. Whatever comes up, you can slash it, defeat it, and keep moving forward. Whether your approach to dating and relationships is with the defensive shield or the offensive sword, neither approach is better than the other. They each come with pitfalls and things you should be aware of.

Shields

No one would argue that the older you get the more you utilize the shield approach to dating. You've had more experiences. And given that you're still single, it means that your past relationships came to an end, be it a peaceful one or all-out warfare. This metaphorical shield could be a primary reason why you perceive that you've become undateable. The more academic lingo for this is called self-sabotage. By definition, self-sabotage is when you unknowingly, or subconsciously, destroy the relationship. It's like drinking poison but hoping it kills the other person. Yikes! Harsh words, right? But this phenomenon is real, and you may be your own worst victim of this. Here are some signs of overusing that trusty shield in your current and past relationships:

1. You wear that devil on your shoulder. That voice telling you something is wrong and you should be careful.

2. You always seem to be the one to exit the relationship. You later question the abrupt decision but then convince yourself it was for the better—for the both of you—because ultimately it wasn't going to work out anyway.

3. You began the relationship with your values intact and felt compatible with the other person initially, only to later find faults in the person (that you knew early on), but now you've decided that they bother you enough to break up.

4. You make a list of the person's faults or instances when you didn't agree on something. You may actually journal these things on your smart phone and put a date next to them so you can randomly look back to analyze a pattern.

5. You're having a great day, and when you get together with your partner later in the day you feel "off"; and for no reason at all, you're all of a sudden at odds with each other—if not a full-blown argument—and have no clue how the argument even started.

6. You use words like, "Well, at least I don't _(fill in the blank)_ to you."

7. One of your greatest weapons is to punish the other person by using avoidance, silent treatment, or ghosting.

8. You intentionally waited for the other person to say "I love you" before you said it.

9. The relationship started out with lots of quality time together, and now you're just not as motivated to spend as much time with that person. You make excuses such as working late, being tired, have errands to run, or just about anything to limit the amount of time you spend with that person today, tomorrow, or several days in a row.

10. There are some things you want to do with that person but some things you don't.

11. When in a debate or argument, you are uncompromising and totally focused on being heard, outsmarting the other person, and ultimately winning the dispute.

12. Some days that person is the greatest thing ever, and other days you feel that they are not in the same universe as you.

13. You bring up past relationships at the wrong times, and you tell yourself you shouldn't—but you just can't help yourself.

Listen, friends, I wrote that short list of items in just a few minutes—and I could keep going—but you get what I'm saying. Using your shield at the right or wrong time isn't the issue; it's when you use it constantly that it becomes an issue. Being guarded and cautious as a new relationship unfolds is healthy and recommended, but learning to holster that big ole Viking shield is smart if you plan on staying with that person long term. It doesn't matter if the person you're dating is a "shield" or a "sword," because either way there's going to be a lot of clashing in the arena, and ultimately, nothing is going to be accomplished. If all you do is walk around with your shield out in front of you, it might as well be the bars of a jail cell you've locked yourself inside of and thrown away the key . . . with no hope of escape.

Swords

There are two sides to every coin, and the flip side of the shield wielder is the crafty swordsman. You are a person that persists. You never say die. Dammit, you love this person you're in a relationship with. No matter what, you're all in, and you're going to fight tooth and nail to keep this great thing together. You have an indomitable spirit, and it has served you well in your career, your parenting, and in your past relationships too—or has it? Here are some signs of overusing that sharp sword in your past relationships:

1. You wear that angel on your shoulder. That voice telling you that everything will work out for the better and that you should charge ahead to victory.

2. You're not afraid to engage with the other person on any lev-

el, be it for good or for bad. You believe that fighting through tough issues leads to a victory for everyone. Hell, half the fun of fighting is the make-up sex afterward. You believe that the hotter the fire, the sharper the blade. Pressure makes diamonds, baby; and your relationship is going to be the biggest diamond in history.

3. You believe that your positivity is a lighthouse for your partner, as if to guide them away from the treacherous rocks of relationship shipwreck.

4. You have the right attitude, and your partner is fortunate to have found you in this life, as no one could ever love them as much as you do. It's just not possible!

5. Sure, you're a fierce fighter, and you know that sometimes your words can sting; but, hey, you're being honest, right? I mean, shouldn't being open and honest be a core value of any healthy relationship?

6. You express to your partner using words like, "I do   _(fill in the blank)_   for you all the time."

7. You want to prove to your partner that you're committed and that you're all in all the time, through thick and thin.

8. You are the one that said, "I love you" first in the relationship.

9. Everything you do is for your partner: Your job. Your health. How you dress. Every decision you make is with your partner in mind, first and foremost.

10. You recognize that your partner is a shield, but sometimes you just can't help yourself and you just push and push a top-

ic even when your partner has said "drop it" or "Hey, I need a break to think/feel on this."

11. Because you're the fighter in the relationship, that makes you the captain of the football team. You call the plays during the game and you're always right—even when you're wrong.

Are you a mighty swordsman? That's awesome if you are. The world needs swords just as much as it needs shields, but the important thing to realize in this trumpeting metaphor is that to have a successful anything in life, you have to have the right balance of sword and shield. A great offense is a great defense, right? Knowing which you are and which one your partner is will help you understand each other in those moments when the going gets tough and if either of you are pushing the self-sabotage envelope of relationship failure over something that potentially is a growth moment and not a self-destruct button.

What you probably noticed after reviewing both of those lists is that you exhibit attributes of both, and that's simply because no one is absolutely one over the other but rather a combination. The thing about human nature is that we can subconsciously become what we need to be, given a certain situation. During moments of intense dialogue between two people, whether they are romantically involved or not, is that the sword and shield can come out at different times during the course of a heated debate. It can even present itself depending on certain topics. During one conversation, both people can wield swords at the same time, while during a different topic you both can display shield behaviors. Ultimately, your personality will lean more toward one behavior over the other.

What this really boils down to is that some people either run away from pain (shield) or run toward pleasure (sword). Both are equally bonafide subconscious strategies.

What this really boils down to is that some people either run away from pain (shield) or run toward pleasure (sword). Both are equally bonafide subconscious strategies. But anything done in the subconscious isn't as reliable and effective toward relationship communication as when you recognize who you are and what your partner is, and you consciously run toward the same thing.

Ms. My True Love

We had similar upbringings. Our core values were compatible, we loved doing the same things together, and we were the best of friends. She was my girl and I was her guy. We had a beautiful dance in our life together that was well balanced between our careers versus the time we spent together. In nearly all aspects we were perfect together, and we had what it took to go the distance. I can't even remember us ever having a single argument—and we dated a long time. She was a sword and I was a shield. Put another way, with more intentional romance, she was our sword and I was our shield. We were a team! The longer we dated the better it seemed. Then the voices started. That ugly demon on my shoulder shrieked in my ear like an annoying parrot. I tried so hard to shut it off, but I just couldn't help myself. Was she the right one? I mean, could I do better? Could she do better than me? I didn't think so. Did she deserve me? Rather than enjoying our dance,

I was now looking for whenever she tripped and then seized the opportunity to highlight it—if only mentally in my own head, like making a list of her faults and mistakes. I never stopped listening to her, but now it was different. It was like I was studying her to see if she met my criteria of what I was looking for, even though I knew she did. What the heck was wrong with me? I love this girl; why am I being so defensive about everything? It was like I was waiting for the worst to happen, even though it never did.

I started having jealous thoughts and being less engaged in conversation. When we met up, I behaved as if it was an obligatory visit rather than a fun and exciting date night. I was in a funk and couldn't get out. Men, this girl would actually run and jump on me and kiss me profusely all over my face when she saw me—just like in the movies. What the hell was wrong with me? I was self-sabotaging this relationship on a subconscious level, and I was clueless as to why. Most of the time, I justified my thoughts based upon other people's relationship failures—not because of our own experiences as a couple and not even based upon my own past unresolved resentments.

Conclusion: I broke up with her, and she married the next guy she dated. They're together to this day, many years later! The "inner me" is the "enemy," and I self-sabotaged a relationship that was with perhaps the greatest woman God has ever put in my life. Make no mistake, I royally messed this up. It's on me!

When someone breaks up with you for no real reason, it isn't the worst thing that can happen. The worst thing is when you're the one that canceled a great thing for yourself and with no rational justification. Not understanding whether you're a mighty swordsman or a mighty shield will lead to self-sabotage in your dating relationship. Whether your relationship is three weeks old or thirty years old, if you don't address your self-sabotaging tendencies on both a conscious and subconscious level, you're destined to repeat your past behaviors well into your future. Stop the madness, get deep with yourself, read every self-help book you can, take a solo weekend trip to wine country, smoke some weed, get in a good church, commit to daily prayer, do as much counseling as is needed, and do whatever you need to do to graduate to a level of introspective consciousness before you lose the greatest thing that may ever happen in your life!

Listen, friends, I'm writing this chapter with blinding tears flooding down my cheeks to the point that I can barely see as I write each word. Do this work now, because if you don't, you're going to carry this manure into the next relationship and all future relationships. Nothing good is going to grow from it. It's only going to exponentially intensify with each love lost and subconsciously perpetuate your undateable tendencies over and over again. Just do it!

CHAPTER 10

Live Strong, Live Long

This chapter hits home with me more than any other. In my earlier career, I had a fantastic job working for a company that specialized in mergers and acquisitions. I had a title, I had a great paycheck (for a twenty-something-year-old); and I was busy checking off all of life's boxes. I bought a house, I got married, I had children, I bought my first new car. Check, check, check. Busy Bobby was checking all the boxes, and the world was applauding! By the time I was twenty-nine, I was already teeing up my first heart attack. I was over three hundred pounds and couldn't even do one pushup without falling on my knees. I was eating in excess of five thousand calories per day, and that was typically all at one sitting. I was working long hours, and my stress level was at an absolute max. To drown out my borderline obesity, my crippling stress, and my general disdain for life, I turned to alcohol nearly every night before bed. I would drink one-quarter to one-half a bottle of liquor daily. It's how I tuned the world out and put myself to sleep.

During this loathsome stretch of my life, I also began having psoriasis sores from head to toe. Once it started, it got worse and worse. I would go to the dermatologist twice a month to receive dozens of steroid shots under my skin to help curb my disgusting plaque spots. I would wear what I called my "blood pajamas" to the doctor. I called them that because after each visit, the entry point of the needle from all the shots would bleed out from the Band-Aids and penetrate through my clothes. I remember one particular occasion I was getting on the elevator after leaving the doctor's office, and there was an elderly couple already on the elevator. When I stepped inside, they took one look at the psoriasis all over my face and the blood spots seeping through my clothes, and they quietly moved as far to the other side of the elevator as they could, and wouldn't make eye contact. It was like I was a leper that was going to infect them. From what my gut was telling me they got off the elevator before their floor.

As was custom, I drove home to shower before changing clothes to head off to the office for work. I stepped out of the shower and just stared at myself buck naked in the mirror. This was my life's "man in the mirror" moment. I hated what I saw. I hated myself. I hated everything about my life, and I knew I had to make a change—a radical and immediate change—or I was headed toward an early grave. This was not the husband I was supposed to be. This was not the dad my children deserved. This was not the man I was raised to be!

That happened in November 2004. That very next week, I went to my town's newly built recreation center. I walked up to the front desk and asked if they had any fitness classes for adults. The lady slid a flyer across the counter, and on it was a class schedule for civilian boot camp. I signed up on the spot and started class at 5:00 a.m. that following Monday. This was my new beginning!

Not only did these classes suck, they were every morning at 5:00 a.m., five days a week. Staying up late to drown my sorrows in liquor was no longer an option. The drill instructors were two super-fit gals that loved to torture the class by beginning each morning with a one-mile run, no matter how cold, hot, rainy, or even sleeting rain. This was boot camp baby, and there were no excuses. The drill instructors kept a daily log of attendance, and if you missed a day, you paid for it. Trust me! If you missed several classes, well, let's just say it was better to just not show up again. It was grueling.

I stayed in that class over five years, and it marked the beginning of my fitness journey that is alive and well to this day. That class taught me a couple of things: First, it showed me that no matter how successful I was outside those four walls, it didn't matter. It did not matter how much money I made, what my name was, or how difficult it was for me to show up just because I was virtually a single parent. Nobody made me sign up; nobody cared. Do the darn workout or get the heck out!

It was expensive too! It was a great business model, to be honest, because if you charge "too much" for the class, it keeps people coming to class each day. There was no pain in walking away from twenty bucks for a six-week class. They wanted you to know you were making an investment.

The second and harshest reality of all was that I discovered just how far I had let myself go. I had people twice my age that had been in the class awhile who were running circles around me. I also noted one of the most awesome things about this class was the camaraderie between the recruits and the daily encouragement that everyone gave to each other, including me. The friendships, both socially and professionally, that I developed in that class are still alive and well in my life today. That daily dose of positivity combined with a grueling workout was what we all needed to start our day, every day. It's what I needed in my life. In fact, I met one of my best friends in that class, and we are still besties to this day.

The fitness industry is astronomical, and it hasn't even come close to climaxing. It's big business. If you don't notice all the fitness-focused content on social media, infomercials, gyms on every corner of your town, then you're just brain dead. We live in the most health-conscious society the world has ever seen. If you're thinking about your health, how you want to lose a few pounds, maybe put on some lean muscle, then you've literally never been better able to accomplish that goal than you are today. There is simply no excuse—other than sheer laziness—not to be in good shape. I'm not saying you gotta have a Tony Horton P90X beach body, but you do owe it to yourself to be a work in progress starting today. No matter where your fitness journey takes you, it starts with one small step.

So how does this relate to this undateable dilemma that plagues society today? Chances are good that the people you know who are happily dating are also happily involved with a gym, a fitness class, or even just doing their own thing in the basement, garage, or right smack in the living room of their home. When you commit to being a healthier version of yourself, you're also committing to being a better person in life. I don't care what your starting point is; the key is to just get started. Doing anything works; doing nothing does not work! Be consistent. When you decide to level up on this crucial part of your life, you will lose weight, your clothes will fit better, and it will spill over into every aspect of your life. Your approach to everything will be better! You'll sleep better, you'll work better, and best of all, your relationships will improve. All of a sudden, people will be interested in what you've got going on and what you're doing. Your conversations will be less mundane, and you'll find that you have a new circle of like-minded friends. But I'm biased on *how* to start this journey, and I want to give you some solid advice that I know works. I've given it to dozens of men and women in the past sixteen years, and it's proven to work time and time again. Here it is: Get in a workout class and surround yourself with others on the same journey. If you're shy, that's fine. Joining a group workout class doesn't mean you have to be Ms. Congeniality. You can go to class, do your thing, then leave. Give it time. Let it grow on you. Let the results do the talking. Throw away your dang scale. Literally put it in the trash can and never look at it again. The numbers don't matter at this point. What matters is how you feel and how your clothes fit. Do not join a gym and download some stupid workout from the internet and try to tackle this alone. The fitness industry isn't huge because people do it alone all the time. It's huge because a lot of well-educated people have discovered the fountain of youth found only in exercise and nutrition—and it starts with being shown and instructed on how to work out and how to eat properly. Nearly all gyms today have group classes with a wide range of interests and fitness levels. Experiment with a few and stick to one that you enjoy more than one that makes you sweat your butt off. Have fun, be consistent, and commit to the journey for at least one year. Your future self will love you for it.

Next, let's talk about eating habits. *No, not that, Bobby,* I can hear you saying to yourself. Get in a group class first and give your body time to acclimate. The next natural step is to begin thinking about what you eat. Food is fuel. Would you pour a bag of potato chips, cookies, candy, or soda in a race car? Hell no, you wouldn't! You'd put the right fuel in so that you can optimize your car's performance—and your body is no different. Start thinking of your body as a machine. You will get out of your machine what you put into it. It's that simple. Can you eat some deep-fried chicken wings with three beers? Heck yes, you can. You just can't do it every day anymore.

Being healthy isn't just about putting your best possible foot forward in the dating world; it's about living strong so that you can live long!

Being healthy isn't just about putting your best possible foot forward in the dating world; it's about living strong so that you can live long! It's about living life to your fullest and being happy with where you are compared to where you came from, and looking forward to where you're going. After one year of exercising and eating healthy, you are no longer "doing a thing"; you are now engaged in a lifestyle that's forever an undeniable part of your future. I hate to be so blunt, but I just have to say it: "Healthy people are happy people, and unhealthy people are unhappy people. Period!" It's a fact, and everyone on the face of the earth knows it. So, are you happy with your health? Are you happy with where you're going? Make this your "man in the mirror" moment, and get going on your fitness journey. More than anything else in this book, this you'll thank me for. I promise!

Let's take a moment to think about what fitness means. Being fit doesn't mean you have to be a certain weight, fit into a certain-size dress, or be able to run the mile in a certain amount of time. It doesn't mean you have big biceps or that perfectly shaped peach-like butt. What it means is that you're physically moving your body and eating the right things to fuel your future progress toward small, attainable fitness goals. Make an attainable goal for yourself, reach that goal, and then set a new goal. Give yourself permission to graduate in small steps along this journey and don't negatively compare yourself to those who are at a higher level because they've been doing it longer or have different goals. If you're exercising and eating healthy foods, then you're achieving your goal! Be happy with your progress and keep reaching for the next level. You know it'll be worth it. If you have a "dad bod," make it a strong "dad bod," and keep pushing! If you have a pooch because every woman in your family is born with it, or because you've birthed children, then put in the work to make it the best it can be. Focus your attention on the areas of your body you can work on and keep pushing. Choosing a healthy lifestyle has just as much to do with accepting what you're born with and how to make it the best it can be as it does making yourself attractive for the dating pool by being strong and healthy. When you commit to a healthy lifestyle, you're also committing to being the best version of yourself. That, ladies and gentlemen, makes you very dateable—not undateable! Live strong, live long, and enjoy the journey!

CHAPTER 11

Stop Picking Up and Eating Bread Crumbs

When you get an itch, what do you do? You scratch it! And when you scratch that one little spot, what do you do next? You scratch a much bigger area because it feels good, right? It's a silly example to relate to dating, but this type of thing is very common in dating as well. You've been single and without a date for a while, and you just get that itch. It's the fourth month in a row, and all you've done is sit at home and do your gym routine, grocery shopping, yard work, laundry, check on your social media—and it's only 3:00 p.m. You're like, "Huh, wonder what I'll do tonight?" Then the itch sets in! You think, "I wish I had made plans earlier in the week," or "Guess I could text someone and see what they're up to." And that's quickly followed by the decision not to because you don't want to seem desperate. Then that's followed by, "Well, hell, I'm going to anyway," which you do. Then you get turned down, because sensible people make weekend plans well in advance. Then you feel stupid and you give up. Next thing you know, you're sitting on your sofa eating microwave popcorn and drinking your favorite bottle of wine all by your lonesome. This undateable behavior goes on for weeks, months, and even years.

You finally get your act together and have weeks where you go on many dates, only to discover that it's a futile attempt to fool yourself that you're being romantically productive. In reality, however, you're just giving yourself a distraction at best, and you're doing so by picking up little bread crumbs and eating them to pacify your starvation. Ugh! Who does this crap? You do, and so do millions of single people all around the world. With dating apps and social media, the ability to keep walking around and around this revolving door has become all too easy.

If this is your preferred dating system, then that's 100 percent fine. Just know that eventually you'll have burnout, quickly followed by weeks or months of recharging, only to do it all over again. Next thing you know, five years of your life has flown by, and you have no real relationship status other than the one you started with—single! Not to mention, you'll likely have those strings of three- to six-month relationships along the way that ended badly and have caused you even more resentment and discouragement, even when you knew deep down that the relationship wasn't going anywhere to begin with. But your "in-it-to-win-it" positive attitude kept you in the relationship thinking that the other person would catch up or change their ways or that perhaps you'd even change for the other person. Listen, everyone knows staying in a relationship hoping someone is going to change is total insanity. Sure, it happens, but on average it doesn't. Staying in that relationship hoping your persistence is going to win out in the end is a waste of time. Is the distraction you so desperately want to scratch worth the investment of your precious time? No, it is not! Do you want to keep picking up and eating bread crumbs or do you want to have the whole loaf of bread and have it your way? If your answer is "Yes," let's talk about what to stop and start doing.

Step One: If you're in a friends-with-benefits (FWB) relationship with one or more people, I'm sorry to tell you that no matter how you think that's going to suffice your needs in lieu of an actual relationship, it's just not going to happen. Here's why: It's not real! FWBs are a drug; and in the best-case scenario, when it's time for it to end, everyone parts peacefully with the friendship intact. In the worst case, it will lead to one of you wanting more than just the sex, and the other one doesn't come around. This often leads to an abrupt and unexplainable ending with a mountain of hurt feelings and resentment. Not to mention your drug dealer rode off into the sunset with someone else, and you had no clue what was happening and never saw it coming. Or maybe, you're the drug dealer, got bored, and started looking for your next addict. Either way, nobody wins in the end.

If you're in a FWB relationship, you're either the drug dealer or the addict; and yes, you can be both. If you've been there, done that, then you know exactly what I'm talking about. If you're unfortunate enough to have been either the drug dealer or the addict, then either way you also know what I'm talking about. Pause for a moment and stop reading right here. Close your eyes and think about the time that you were either the drug dealer or the addict and how it all came crashing down. Has it happened only once or has it happened many times in your past? Plus, here's the part that really sucks: If you are the one that gets the memo that things are about to abruptly end and your drug supply is at an end, what do you do? You find a new drug dealer so you can keep up the routine of pushing that metaphorical sex needle into your veins to get that high you so desperately think you need because you're addicted. I'm no clinical psychologist, but I know enough to inform you that a FWB faux relationship has nothing to do with "how much" or "how often" you're taking this drug, but rather what your level of dependence is on the drug dealer who's feeding you what you're convinced you need to survive. Regardless, one thing is for sure: The more regular your FWB drug use is, then it's an even more-sure sign you're addicted. Here's the deal: Just like an actual drug addiction, if you're living that life, then you're most certainly not living mentally healthy. When that happens for a long enough period of time, you're causing irreparable damage to your mental health because your emotional IQ is tanking! It's like drowning in a tank of water where only one drop falls every few seconds. You're drowning so slowly you can't even tell you're running out of oxygen. Here's what you gotta do: QUIT! Boom, it's that simple! Now, even I know from experience that saying something is "simple" doesn't mean it's "easy"—especially when it comes time to quit a bad habit cold turkey. There is no nicotine patch for this drug to slowly taper yourself off! It's cold turkey or not at all. My FWB friends, this is gonna hurt, and it's gonna be messy at best! Even if you part ways as friends, it will certainly have the momentum to keep going. In a very short amount of time, you'll quickly find yourself right back in the same drug house; that is, you have to go through the pain of doing the breakup all over again. This is the type of drug where you have to metaphorically check yourself into rehab and be prepared to stay until you're clean. You can't just slam the brakes on a moving train and expect it to stop where you want it to. You have to lay dynamite on the tracks, push the detonate button and just deal with the mess the explosion causes as best you can. Sorry y'all; wish I had better advice.

This is the type of drug where you have to metaphorically check yourself into rehab and be prepared to stay until you're clean. You can't just slam the brakes on a moving train and expect it to stop where you want it to. You have to lay dynamite on the tracks, push the detonate button and just deal with the mess the explosion causes as best you can. Sorry y'all; wish I had better advice.

I wish I could introduce you to some simple 12-step program on how to carry out this process, but there isn't one. You've simply got to make up your mind to quit and then execute. However, I will give you some solid words of advice, a "script" to go by that will help you—at a minimum—to organize your thoughts on how to pull this Band-Aid off quickly. I do suggest that you do this in person, as it has more impact. This isn't something you do over a text, and you should only do this over the phone if you feel that the other person will lose their cool and be pissed off, or even aggressive. Here it is: "Jim, listen. I hate to tell you this because we have spent so much time together, but I need to bring our FWB relationship to an end. I know this may be a shock, but I need to do some "self-work" on myself, and the only way I'm going to do this is to abstain from sex right now. Please don't take this personally! This is about 'me' wanting to make some changes in my life." Notice I didn't suggest that you offer an apology. There is no need to apologize. Does a drug addict apologize to his drug dealer for no longer buying drugs from him? No! A true FWB relationship is just shy of a business arrangement anyway. If you don't want to keep doing business with that company, you simply quit spending your money, right? This is no different. It's time to stop spending your physical and emotional dollars on something (or someone) that doesn't provide any real value. Your drug dealer may act mad, cry, or even beg. But there's something common among all drug dealers: They'll find someone new to sell to. Remember, you're ready to take your unfair share of that hot and fresh loaf of bread right out of the oven and smother it with butter and your favorite jelly. Stop eating the crumbs!

Step Two: Get your mind and your body right! That means get healthy physically, mentally and, most of all, emotionally. Read. Pray. Eat Right. Join a workout group. Go to church. Meditate. Get counseling. Attend a mental-health conference. Journal. Learn breathing techniques. Bottom line: Give yourself permission to have a growth mindset, and then go do it! Do what you gotta do—and only you know what that is—and whatever that is, get started and give it the necessary time it needs to bear the right fruit. Regardless of what your action plan is to accomplish all you need to do, there is one particular thing that you simply must do to kick-start this process. You know that all-too-supportive friend you have that you haven't spent enough time with or have been ignoring their calls or have been less than engaged with? It's now time to engage with intention. Maybe it's not just one person; maybe it's a small group of friends, a church group, social club, civic organization, workout group, pistol club, bike club, motorcycle club, or perhaps even your own family members. The key is this: It must be a person or group that's positive, supportive, accepting, and understanding. You must be able to communicate where you're at and where you're going, and know they have your back and are going to be on and by your side.

This isn't a disposable lighter that you pick up and put down only when you need it. If that's been your habit historically, it's time to correct that. This person or group is going to be permanent. Sure, it will evolve over time, but it's going to be a foundational stone in your life. Whatever you choose, you should be passionate about it. It should be something (or someone) that you not only look forward to, but someone you will find yourself planning ahead to associate with. These days, this step is really important to take because social media has made it easier than ever to connect with like-minded groups of people that are semi or fully organized. Roll your sleeves up, get in there, have fun rediscovering your long-lost passion, and don't be afraid to try something new. The quality of the person or group is far more important than the activity you engage in.

Step Three: When the time is right, figure out how *you* want to date. You are the main character in your play. You are the star, and that means you dictate how the script of your life is written. If you want to find a worthy costar, then it's not really about finding Mr. Right or Ms. Right; it's about finding someone that has the same script as you. I know that sounds like a bunch of overreaching, metaphorical psychobabble. It's not. Trust me! The Law of Attraction is real, and what you put into the ether will come back to you. I've simply lived too long and have too many real examples from my life that prove it's true. I tell my work groups all the time, "If you want to be terrific, you have to be specific." And in that spirit, I want to challenge you to actually pause for a few minutes and do this simple exercise: Grab a piece of paper, open your laptop (or use your smartphone notes), and I want you to describe your perfect one-year relationship. YIKES! I want you to be specific so that you'll be terrific! Start with how you met, your first date, your first kiss, hug, touch, words, tears, argument. Describe all your "firsts" from the first year, and get down and dirty with details whenever you can. This is not a bullet-point list; this is a specific exercise where you will write your script for your next relationship. Listen closely, my friends. Don't take this exercise lightly. This is your script. What you write here is going to happen, so take it seriously. Your subconscious is recording every word and every emotion of what you're writing down and putting it out to the universe. Once it's out there, it's a finished product of what you expect and what you want going forward. To help you get started, I'll go first . . .

Ms. Professor

Her name was Rachel. She didn't know me, I didn't know her, and we had no friends in common. She popped up on my social media as someone I might know. I clicked on her profile and did the proverbial scrolling all the way back to the beginning of when she joined Facebook in 2009. She was younger than me but not by too much. She was smart, had a perfect smile, and a fun sense of style on how she dressed. She loved hats! All types of hats. She was successful and professional but still very much the "girl next door." She looked great dressed up. Even her pictures from that hunting trip where she was wearing camo really got my attention. I love to hunt and fish and do all things outdoors, and all her pictures doing those things really spoke to me. She has kids about the same age as mine, and she's been divorced for about the same amount of time as me. I noticed that during her divorce she didn't spew ugly nonsense all over her social media about how crappy her ex-husband was or how disastrous her dire situation was. For the most part, she was relatively silent on the matter, other than a few posts about how she's growing and learning and staying positive. The pictures with her kids, family, and friends are very genuine and don't appear staged as if for a photo opportunity. She's a city girl now but grew up with a spiritual foundation and, like me, in a small town. Both of her parents are very much a part of her life, and they, too, look happy, healthy, and have been happily married for years.

I tap the button to send her a friend request and then forget all about it. Several days go by, and I notice her posts start showing up in my social media feed. She doesn't post every hour of the day, just a few times a week. Her posts are always upbeat, positive, and thoughtful. Ugh, that perfect smile had me going crazy! Plus, she's got a healthy body, and she clearly takes the right steps to stay that way. I check to see if she accepted my friend request. She hasn't. Duh! Of course she hasn't! A girl like that gets friend requests by the dozens every week. No biggie. Maybe she'll accept and maybe she won't. Regardless, I do enjoy seeing her posts and having little daydream fantasies about what our first date would be like or whether we'd have fun together just being friends.

Several months go by, and I haven't looked at her profile in a while—outside of seeing her posts that come up occasionally. I click on her profile and scroll back to when I first noticed her. Doesn't appear to be any signs of a relationship. I checked on my friend request, and it's still there. Just sitting there. I clicked the button to delete it. Clearly she's seen it a few times by now and has just chosen not to accept it. No biggie. The universe gives and it takes away. *Onward and upward,* I think to myself.

A few hours later, a very unexpected notification pops up on my social media account. Rachel sends me a friend request and a direct message! I'm shocked, I'm pumped, and I'm so confused. Does she even realize I sent her a friend request like a year ago? Needless to say, I go to my messaging account and open it up. Her message reads . . . Rachel: "Hey there, Bobby! I saw one of your posts a few days ago about what women need to do to strengthen their arms and shoulders, and it was super helpful. I've always felt like my arms were not strong enough, and I'm always trying new things to make them look more svelte. Thanks for sharing."

Bobby: "Well, hello there, Rachel. Wow, I was so surprised to get a friend request from you. I accepted it. I love your posts because they're always positive, and you have a killer smile in all your photos. So yeah, I'm not a personal trainer or anything, but I have a small fitness group I'm an admin for on social media that specifically addresses both men and women's physical fitness and things of that nature."

Rachel: "Oh wow. What's the group's name? I'll check it out."

Bobby: "@LockerRoomSTL. I live here in St. Louis, so it's mostly based out of this area. Hey, I have a funny question to ask you, if that's ok."

Rachel: "Sure! What's up?"

Bobby: "Not sure if you noticed, but I sent you a friend request a very long time ago and actually had just deleted it, only to find you sent one to me along with your message. Could you tell I deleted the friend request?"

Rachel: "You mean the friend request you sent me like a year ago?" (haha emoji)

Bobby: "Um, yeah, that one!" (haha emoji) "Honestly, I didn't think you even noticed. You're a very attractive girl, and I just figured that you get friend requests from single guys all the time, and you just ignore them."

Rachel: "Yes, I do. And yes, you're right, I ignore them. But I've been watching your posts for some time now, and I have just been admiring from afar." (eek emoji)

Bobby: "What's the matter, you chicken?" (chicken emoji) "Haha. JK. Guess you just wanted to make the first move, huh?"

Rachel: "Well, yes and no! And no, I'm not a chicken; just a busy gal and a bit shy when it comes to social media and reaching out to people. I keep my 'friends' at a minimum and typically only accept a friend request if it's someone I know or have met and am connecting with for a genuine friendship."

Bobby: "Gotcha! Totally makes sense. Everyone does it differently. I totally get where you're coming from and wanting to play it safe. Social media is fun, but it can be creepy if you're not careful. Same is true for me, but I think pretty girls definitely have to have their guard up more so than men."

Rachel: ("100" emoji) "I found that page and gave it a 'like.' So you live in St. Louis, huh? Cool. I've been there a few times for work. It's a neat city—and who doesn't like the Cardinals, right?"

Bobby: "Yup! Been here twenty years now. I love it here. Plus, I grew up in the Midwest so I decided at a young age to stay here. Well, because you sent me a friend request and you only 'friend' people that you want to be a real friend with, I guess that makes us 'real' friends now?!" (haha emoji)

Rachel: "Well, ok, if you insist. But if you send me a dick pic, I'm cutting it off and mailing it to you!"

Bobby: (haha emoji) "OK, that's hilarious. And 'no,' I won't be sending you any dick pix, Rachel. So listen, I have a small confession to make; is that ok?"

Rachel: "Oh boy, what's that? Don't get weird on me. Remember what I'll do!" (eek emoji)(haha emoji)

Bobby: "I sent you that friend request all those months ago after you popped up on my feed as someone I might know. I totally creeped your profile and loved your personality so I thought I'd shoot you a friend request. I, too, am not one to do that, but you really caught my eye, and I figured you were totally worth my attention." (eek emoji)(four-leaf clover emoji)(green heart emoji)

Rachel: "Hmm! So you are a social media stalker after all, huh?"

Bobby: (haha emoji) "Ha! As if! Not at all. Just the opposite! Just a simple guy in the world who noticed a beautiful smile and thought I'd connect and say hello! I didn't have any intentions other than a simple online connection and let the universe take it from there."

Rachel: "Yeah? How'd that work for ya?" (haha emoji) "JK. You're fine!"

Bobby: "You're such a brat. Li'l bit sassy, aren't ya?!"

Rachel: "M-A-Y-B-E!" (haha emoji)(angel emoji)(devil emoji)

Bobby: "Well then, introductions are made, and we've clearly identified that I dropped the ball and wasn't persistent enough! Right? Rhetorical question! Well, I won't let that happen again!

I see from your profile that you live in TX. Not sure what the prospects are of us meeting in person due to the distance, but I'm thrilled that we're connected now."

Rachel: "Yeah. We live pretty far apart, but who knows. I gotta get back to work, but if you're ever this way, or I'm that way, we should keep in touch. Sound good?"

Bobby: "Of course. Let's do that! Talk soon."

This communication continues on and off again for weeks on end, then . . .

Rachel: "Hey, Mr. Fit Cute Guy From STL!" (haha emoji) "I wanted to let you know that I will be in St. Louis next month for a couple days for a work-related assignment!"

Bobby: "Well, hello, Ms. Professor! Really! That's awesome. It's beautiful this time of year. We don't have Texas's bluebonnets, but the magnolia trees here are gorgeous in the spring. When are you coming?"

Rachel: "Haha! 'Ms. Professor.' Not totally sure on the exact dates yet, but I'll let you know."

Bobby: "Hey Rachel. I have an important question to ask you."

Rachel: "What's up?"

Bobby: "May I take you on a date?"

Rachel: "I thought you'd never ask!"

Bobby: "Is that a 'yes?'"

Rachel: "*Y*E*S*."

Her plane landed, and she was staying at a downtown hotel. Her work detail was at St. Louis University on Thursday and Friday. She extended her trip for the weekend— she didn't say why—and I didn't ask nor assume anything. We made a plan to meet up Saturday afternoon about 3:00 p.m..

Three Sixty Rooftop was a swanky restaurant/bar in downtown St. Louis that overlooked Busch Stadium where the St. Louis Cardinals play and had an awesome view of the world-famous St. Louis Arch. I couldn't think of a better place to meet this incredible gal that I've been talking to online for months on end. The weather was perfect, so I rode my Harley-Davidson to go and meet her. I had noticed on one of her social media profiles that she enjoyed riding motorcycles, so I thought maybe, just maybe if things went well, she'd hop on the back and I'd take her around downtown a bit. We could head down to the cobblestone riverfront walkway in front of the Arch for some fun conversation and, if things went really well, maybe even a couple of pictures in front of the arch. I planned the perfect date night!

Three Sixty is on the rooftop of the Hilton Hotel next to Ballpark Village, and we agreed to meet in the lobby by the front doors. I walked in, and much to my surprise, she was standing right there waiting for me. She was holding two fresh cups of Starbucks coffee. We shared a quick hug with lots of eye contact, and she handed me my favorite Starbucks drink, a cold caramel ribbon crunch. Several weeks ago we had this long conversation about how much we loved coffee, and I was astonished that she remembered what my favorite was. Wow, I was so impressed! I even told her, and she was immediately sassy with me, "Well, yeah. What did you think all this conversation was for? Of course I remembered your favorite." Gestures like this aren't typically the type of thing that make me swoon, but what could I say? I was smitten with this "Lil Trixie" from Austin Texas, and this totally seemed like something she'd do.

We stood there for a couple of minutes just chatting about her trip and drinking our coffee. The eye contact and immediate chemistry was exhilarating. It was a perfect first-time meeting and introduction. My heart was pounding, and I swear I could even feel the sweat from my armpits running down my side. I was so fired up. We made our way over to the elevator to get up to the rooftop. We entered the elevator—it was just the two of us with twenty-five floors to go. She stood on one side of the elevator and I stood on the other. We looked at each other for what seemed like forever; then we both started laughing because we were both thinking the same thing: "Why are we standing so far apart from each other?" It was so funny! Without saying a word, we both began to take one large step toward each other at exactly the same moment, and we met right in the middle. We were face to face, and both of us were smiling ear to ear. Not a word was spoken, but OMG, it was so intense! It was one of those awkward moments where I didn't know if I wanted to just keep smiling like the Cheshire Cat or, just to shock her, plant a big ole kiss right on her mouth when she didn't expect it. The elevator chimed and the door opened. Dammit! I needed two more floors to seal this deal.

I thought to myself, "Oh, this is going to be so much fun!"

Bobby: "Follow me. I want to show you something really cool." I took her hand, and we walked right out to the rooftop and stood on the east side to view the St. Louis Arch.

Rachel: "Wow, that's so incredible! Thank you for bringing me here!"

Bobby: "It is beautiful, isn't it?"

We finished our coffees and quickly switched to a pair of super fun drinks from the bar and just walked around the rooftop for awhile. We even watched the sun set over the St. Louis skyline. It was perfect!

We talked forever about anything and everything. The most fun was rehashing all our text messages from the bygone weeks and going back to certain topics to retrace things we had said to each other. We wanted to make sure that what we said was what was actually interpreted by the other. We laughed our asses off. Sometimes we were right on the money, and other times a certain topic was completely misplaced. We sorted everything out effortlessly, and the more we drank the funnier it was.

We had dinner, and she marveled at the world-famous St. Louis T-Ravs (toasted ravioli), which was made famous by Charlie Gitto's, a long-standing restaurant in the area. They were really good!

It was getting late, and I asked her if she fancied a small tour of Downtown St. Louis on the back of my Harley-Davidson. "I thought you'd never ask," she replied. I said, "Do you remember when you first said that to me?" She replied, "Yes, when we first started talking. And I've been on pins and needles since that day." Perfect answer! I thought to myself, *this girl is going to steal my heart, and I have no chance of resisting.*

As luck would have it, Washington Ave. was hosting a live music block party, so we pulled over and watched a live concert while sitting on my bike that was parked illegally. Oh well! We didn't talk. We just watched the band, had several intimate glances and some chance hand touching. Totally innocent, playful touching; but it was like intentionally sticking my hand in an electric panel. The electricity between us was like nothing I've ever experienced. I know she felt the same.

It was midnight. I offered to take her to her hotel but only if she'd let me take her to the riverwalk to see the St. Louis Arch lit up in the night sky. "I thought you'd never ask," she replied. There it is again. I love green lights! (Thank you, Matthew McConaughey).

I parked right on the sidewalk at the bottom of the Arch. We sat there on my bike and just looked at the Mississippi River on our left and the St. Louis Arch on our right. The sky was clear, the air was warm, and it was one of those moments that you consciously press the record button in your head. Moments like this only come along once in a lifetime, and you don't ever want to forget! She pressed her body against my back and put her arms around me and pulled me into her. She whispered in my ear, "This is the best date I've ever been on. Thank you!"

Ok, so you get the idea, right? John 1:1—In the beginning was the Word, and the Word was with God, and the Word was God.

Spending your time thinking about the perfect date, the perfect guy, the perfect girl, the perfect relationship is a worthy exercise that all singles engage in. But when you re-create those visions in the written form, it's like chiseling it on stone tablets. It forces the thinking to a deeper level. It's no longer a vapor in your mind that vanishes a few minutes later. It now becomes a script that you can reference later. It becomes real because it's in black and white. When you expand your mind about what you want, in writing, it will never return to its original form. It's why vision boards are so popular these days! Writing down what your ideal relationship looks like from the very beginning and for several months that follow is worthy of your time.

CHAPTER 12

X-Men

This chapter is for my brothers from another mother! As you've probably gathered by now, I love cinema! I love action, drama, suspense, and pretty much anything on the big screen. Not horror, though; too many bad memories about horror movies from when I was growing up, so I steer away from those types of movies. The same is true in dating; that is, any type of situation can be the right situation for meeting, greeting, and dating—except for the horror situation. Men, what I mean is, you can make the right move at any time when the right opportunity presents itself—and, of course, all people want to avoid the horror movie equivalent of dating. In this short chapter, I want to share with you what all your male friends got wrong and what your daddy never told you. Put your helmet on men; let's ride!

Before I begin, and as I have implied throughout this book, there are no absolutes in dating or in the human condition. But in my experience, I can certainly reflect and share with you what I've encountered in all facets of my life as it pertains to what all women want. They want a man to look, act, smell, work, taste, talk and, most of all, to be a real man! If you're a real man, then this is just about as far as you need to read. But for many men in this day and age, that image of what a real man is has become seriously diluted, confused, made too delicate—and again, I'll repeat—diluted!

Before I really peel this back, let me set the record straight on one thing: Your profession does not determine your manliness. How you approach your life and your actions are what determine whether or not you're a proud man-card-carrying member of the masculine race. If you're the biggest nerd on the planet, you can be a real man. If you make a crap ton of money and don't need to do any actual work yourself on your car or your home, then you can still be a man. Men, please listen carefully: What you do does not determine whether or not you are a real man. The type of clothes you wear, the car you drive, what color you are, your language, what part of town you live in or even if you're gay—none of these things determine your manliness. It is your actions, your posture, your mindset, your work ethic, and your approach to all things "life" that can set you apart in dating no different than in life as a whole. I've known men who are over six foot, drive a big ole truck, have a hairy beard, covered in tats, well built, cuss like a sailor, and they're the biggest wussies I've ever met. Conversely, I've seen men who are quiet, short, average, modest income, and generally perceived as being invisible by society, and they are the biggest contributors to men and what we stand for on the planet. Whatever stereotype or image you think you portray, I want you to start with a clean slate, look deep, and get real with yourself as you continue to read this chapter.

Let me start with the genesis of what makes a man "a man."

It's not just your penis; it's your DNA! These days you can identify however the hell you want—and you can even make radical changes to your body's chemistry and your manhood. But there is one thing that all humans generally have in common, and that is, you're either born a male or a female. Period! If you were born male, then you were genetically designed for a specific purpose—and I don't just mean procreation.

This chapter is about more than that. Men are designed to initiate, and that is what I'm going to focus on first and foremost. You know that age-old expression, "Nice guys finish last?" That's not true! What it should say is, "Men who don't initiate finish last." It is my belief that men are genetically designed to initiate. Men are hunters. Men are designed to grow up, leave the comforts of their childhood, struggle a bit, grow into their survival instincts, and by God, go into the world and make something of themselves. Men are designed to be protectors. If you haven't ever been punched squarely in the face, I encourage you to make that happen—soon! It's humbling, and you will grow from it infinitely. It's just one of many things that'll make a man out of you. Men are designed to be providers. If all you're capable of doing is barely paying your own way in life, then you are undateable. And guess what, you won't be able to fully attract a life mate for very long. If you are able to sustain a long-term relationship, then it simply means that she's even weaker than you are, or worse yet, she's wearing your pants for you.

That's only 23.8 percent of your week that's directed toward your money-making profession. What you do with the other 76.2 percent is what determines what people really think about you.

In this modern economy, we no longer have to spear our food or battle with warring tribes on a daily basis, but men face a different adversary, and that is the ability to "initiate" every single day of the week. If your entire "net worth" is all about your 401(k), then you're missing the meaning to life. There are 168 hours in a seven-day week, and only forty-plus hours of your labor are generally used to make money. That's only 23.8 percent of your week that's directed toward your money-making profession. What you do with the other 76.2 percent is what determines what people really think about you. The lowest common denominator of the human male race is that we are born to initiate. We are born to take the initiative to be agents of change, leaders, protectors, thinkers and, above all else, doers!

I want you to imagine for a moment a multibillionaire Silicon Valley entrepreneur. There's plenty to choose from these days, so just pick one. Think about what that guy looked and acted like when he was a kid, then a young adult. Then within ten to twenty years he's married to a smoking hot chick, big house, cars, world traveler—I think you get the idea. He's the nice guy that finished last, right? Nope, he's not! You see, he took initiative and started something from nothing. He closed his eyes and saw "something" special where others saw "nothing." He faced constant and insurmountable hurdles and struggles, and he persisted. And let me tell you, women find that extremely sexy!

Men, before we talk about *how* to initiate with a woman, you need to make sure your own affairs are in order. In this world today, your wallet is your spear! Do you have a job? If not, that's ok; but are you working toward a bigger goal? Have you been working toward that goal for five years and you're further behind than when you started—including living with your parents, playing video games, drinking too much, and/or haven't been to a gym since high school PE class? Get your life together, my brother, before you forge ahead with any type of intimate relationship with the opposite sex. Here's why: Do you think it's smart to commingle your already-struggling financial affairs while trying to grow a healthy, intimate relationship at the same time? It's a rhetorical question, and deep down you know the right answer. It does not put you in a position of strength, and ultimately it will not put you in the right light with the right woman. This in turn leads you to be with the wrong woman. If you're in any type of secondary education and you're actively working toward your career path, then high five; you're taking initiative to secure yourself financially. If you're working two jobs to get ahead in life, you're on the right track. If you have a high-paying job and are saddled with debt up to your eyeballs because you have a four-thousand-dollar-a-month house payment, a one-thousand-dollar-a-month vehicle payment and fifty thousand dollars or more in credit card debt, then your income doesn't mean spit! Listen, there are enough podcasts, articles, and books out there already on this topic, and as men, we've all heard it before. But are you taking action? You have to be number one in your life until such time you are secure enough financially to make room for more, such as an intimate relationship—not to mention buying a home, having kids and providing for a family, taking fun trips, and saving for the future. If this has kicked your ego in the gut and you feel your entrails falling into your arms as you try to stuff them back into your bloody body cavity, then I've made my point. I'm in no way being subtle about this point! If you want to be undateable and continue to live your life on one-night stands and empty relationships, then just continue to spend more than you make. Your un-dateable future will be set in stone until you get your act together!

Dating is an art form, and faking it until you make it makes about as much sense as pouring laundry detergent into a race car. Trust me; women will see your spitting, sputtering, and stinky, black smoke as you explode off the starting line like a champ, only to have your engine blow up in a fiery blaze in only a few dates. Women have a radar for men's bullcrap, and the woman of your dreams will kick you to the curb eventually—no matter how much she loves you. It's a hard truth, my brothers. Not sorry!

Ok brothers, are we good? Great! Next, let's talk about your approach. While I said that your choice of career doesn't have anything to do with your masculinity, how you approach your everyday life, and specifically your work, is a macro indicator of how you will approach an intimate relationship. If you get up at the same time every day, do the same job all day every day, drive home, eat supper, watch TV, then go to bed, you are definitely a consistent person. I'll give you that. But that's not enough. You're simply a mindless robot going through life day by day, and there's nothing interesting about you.

If you think that because you have no debt, have a good job, can cook for yourself, and do your own laundry secures your po-sition as an independent male, well then, you're right; but that's all you are. You are a consistent, reliable, steady, and undateable drone. When was your last promotion? What are you doing to deserve a promotion? When was the last time you put your re-sume on the market to shop for a better job or invest money in your own company in order to advance yourself? If you are happy with where you are (and your income), that's totally fine. High five on succeeding at your 23.8 percent. But what are you doing with your 76.2 percent? What you do with your time when you're not at work is truly what defines you and how people will think about and remember you. Are you taking initiative or are you simply going through the motions of life doing the minimum and sticking to your routine so as not to ruffle any feathers, salute your many generals at work, and keep your momma proud with your stability? Have you run for city council? School board? Parents as teachers? Started a small group in your church? Reading self-help books? Camping, snowboarding, hiking, shooting skeet, or taking a leadership position in any way at all?

The time for you to act is NOW! Consider this your wakeup call! If you've been praying for a sign from God, this is it! Get off your butt, quit being passive, and stop procrastinating. Go contribute your time, talents, and treasures toward something greater than your own self-serving life. And when you do, a whole new world is going to open up and you will become a member of the X-Men that you are designed to be a part of. You don't have to shoot for the stars; just take one step forward, then the next, and get going.

One of the greatest wrestling coaches of all time would constantly yell at his wrestlers in practice and even right on the mat during a high-stakes duel, "Motion creates opportunity," and it does so every single time. You must initiate! Take massive action! When is a good time to act? Now! Whether you've mastered your 23.8 percent or your 76.2 percent—both or neither—you must always be moving toward personal growth and self-confidence and away from the mundane and the boring. Stay in action. Simply put, your approach to things in your life has everything to do with how you approach the opposite sex when you're moving toward being a fine-ass catch of a man and away from being a low self-esteem, passive and undateable male.

Brothers, I love you with all my heart. And it is because of this agape love that I want to be your mental wingman as you now venture into the deep, dark, and seemingly torturous world of approaching a woman that has captured your gaze, struck your imagination like a bolt of lightning, and has mentally prepared you to surrender all that you are and simply act as your true self. To be your unique, single-power X-Man that only you have the ability to do and that only you can present to her. Being a normal, everyday, average dude that wishes to date means you must have a single superpower, that fingerprint that is uniquely yours and will make you stand out above any man she's ever encountered. Superman had many powers, and he was from another planet, an alien—not a human! The one thing all X-Men have in common is that they are born from humans, yet they have that singular thing that makes them special. That one thing! You are an X-Man! You are gifted. God instilled in you that special ingredient to make you successful at how you approach everything in your life, especially dating.

Take a moment and think about who you are, what you are, and what you've accomplished in your life. Then ask yourself what the common thread is that sewed it all together. This isn't a resume; it's something very small, very simple, and that you could describe in only a few words. Do you have a killer smile? Maybe you are funny or witty? Smart? Handsome? Strong? A cool hobby, sport, or organization you belong to? Hell, maybe you're quirky, nerdy, or even stutter. It doesn't matter what it is. All that matters is that you're convinced of it and that it's genuine to who you are as a man. Unless you're an astronaut, took a bullet for the POTUS or you're the Pope, trust me when I tell you that your X-Man superpower is not your job. Blah! Yuck! Boring! Whatever your job is, she's heard it before! Oh yeah, one quick thing: It's not your kissing ability either, and I don't recommend leading with that as your introduction. I've tried it—a few times actually—and it's a no-go if you want to be taken seriously and not as a philandering playboy that keeps women's panties in his night stand.

One thing I get asked from men often is this: "How do I even initiate a real conversation with someone I'm interested in?" Just for fun, let's analyze this question like this: There are three different levels on how to make conversation with a complete and total stranger of the opposite sex. Just because you can start at a higher level or level up as you go doesn't mean you're going to be more successful. In fact, the more humble you are the more successful you'll be. It all starts with a simple "Hello!"

Face-to-Face Introductions:

Beginner: "Hello! My name is Bobby. What's yours?"

Intermediate: "Hello! I've noticed you for some time now, and even though I'm nervous as hell, I simply could not help myself anymore; I had to come over and introduce myself. My name is Bobby. What's your name?"

Advanced: "Hello! I know you don't know me and must think it takes a lot of guts to come say hello to such a beautiful woman like you; and you're right, it most certainly does. But I have to tell you, the thing that really got my attention about you these last few times I've seen you here is that you stir your coffee the whole time you're drinking it. Did you know that they can "froth" your drink here if you ask them to?" *(Um, ok wow, no, I didn't)* "Yeah, I have them do mine that way. By the way, my name is Bobby. What's yours?"

Dating App Introductions:

Beginner: "Hi! I go by Bobby. I like your profile pic. Why'd you choose that one?"

Intermediate: "Hey, Blondee375! I've seen your profile a couple of times, and I loved the picture of you and your friends on vacation in Austin. How did y'all pick that city for your vacation adventure? Have you been to San Antonio too?"

Advanced: "Hey there, BrownEyes314! Wow! You are an adventurous gal! Me too! I can tell by your profile pictures that you love to travel—and we've even been to some of the same places. I had a super fun time in Nashville. What was your favorite thing to do there? By the way, I love the pic of you in glasses. It definitely shows off the gorgeous brown eyes—not to mention makes you look like a total genius!"

Ok men, that's all the help you need—for now! Perhaps I'll write another book that delves more deeply into the topic of initiating conversation, as well as other things that a man can and is expected to initiate in a relationship. For now, these simple opening lines can get you started on the right foot. Once the conversation starts and/or a date commences, just let it flow naturally. Ask more questions. Make less comments. Don't talk about your lame-ass job. And I'd suggest you don't ask her about hers either until after at least a good twenty minutes of initial conversation. Be yourself; but remember, this is a "new friend," not your buddy you grew up with. Don't talk like a sailor, drink too much, or dominate the conversation. Talk to her like you would your mom, your sister, or even just an earnest friend. Be kind, be considerate, and don't hit the ball until it's your turn—and hit for first base, not a home run. Less is more. Always!

Men, I want to give you this list of things I've identified as the Top 10 things women want in their X-Man. There's no fancy-schmancy study conducted by some big Ivy League school or even a closed focus group of a couple thousand women across all ages or backgrounds. This is *my* list, and I stand by it 100 percent. This list is short, simple, and self-explanatory. Know these things, and you'll be the Wolverine of X-Men.

What She Wants In Her X-Man:

1. He takes initiative in his life and with me.

2. He's handy and can fix common, everyday stuff.

3. He knows how to handle me, handle tough situations, handle a room, and handle his income.

4. He's manly yet vulnerable and open to real intimacy.

5. He's faithful, authentic, honest, and is who he says he is.

6. He's my protector, and he's got my back no matter what; he

would die for me.

7. He understands me and knows what makes me tick.

8. He can communicate with me about everyday things.

9. He knows his words, and his actions back that up.

10. He notices me, is attracted to me, desires me, and sees past my flaws.

And because of all these things, he is 'sexy' in my eyes and worthy of my time, my sacrifice, my commitment, and my body!

CRITICAL NOTE: Men, note that out of the ten items above, some of them are about "him" and some of them are about "her." Women are alluring creatures that way! Get it? Hands down I can tell you from both personal as well as years of observational experience in my career that one of the leading causes of premature relationship failure is also the one thing that's the easiest to address: communication.

Men, I want to genuinely encourage you to try harder. You embrace confrontation in every aspect of your life except in your most intimate relationships. Your excuse of "I have to fight at work so I don't want to fight at home," isn't going to hold water in a long-term relationship. Cancel that mindset permanently! Women use 65 percent more words than men on an average day. The simple truth is that women use their words to communicate vastly more than their male counterpart. In the area of communication, women fight to be understood, and men fight to be heard. It's the proverbial Yin and Yang of relationship communication; and when not understood, it leads to communication breakdown. The thing that makes women feel understood is the exact same thing that leads men to feel heard: the use of words. More specifically, the calm and rational exchange of words between two people who care for each other. They care enough to listen and understand, and they care enough to be patient and to be heard. It's a 50:50 exchange. It's two sides of the same coin. I know how hard it is to bite your tongue so you can listen. I know how challenging it is to want to make something that's emotionally complex appear to be a simple yes or no conversation. Men prefer to take the communication shortcut and get right to the rational conclusion. Women, on the other hand, don't want to pass "GO." They want to place their chip on every square of the emotional Monopoly board and talk it out.

Men, all I can say is this: This dynamic isn't new. It's always been this way, and it will always be this way. If you are all too willing to listen intently to her while you're dating, then the same should hold true in moments of intensity and when communication is critical months into the relationship. Your dad may have told you—or perhaps you even witnessed it while growing up— that your dad would just grit and bear it, then later in life tell you, "It's better to just let her get it out of her system and it'll blow over." But what he really meant to say, hopefully, was that if you really care for her, you'll listen to what she is saying, understand her position, and reply calmly and with care. When it comes to verbal communication, two wrongs don't make a right, and two negatives don't equal a positive. Because men are eager to be heard, that makes them poor listeners when it comes to tense conversation, even when it's not argumentative. Work diligently to overcome that!

When you master this, you'll not only advance your relationship with your gal, but you'll also advance your career by leaps and bounds. When you don't listen intently, it will drive a wedge between the two of you, and both sides will perpetually dig their heels in and butt heads like rams. It's counterproductive and leads to hurt and heartache. And above all else, over long periods of time it will lead to heaping mounds of resentment that not even a bulldozer can level out. The undateable man is said to be short with his words, slow to listen, quick to solve, and insistent on wanting to always be in the position of being right all the time. The very dateable and desirable man is an exquisite listener, feeler, and will work to solve nothing but rather to simply understand.

> *Here's the craziest thing of all: For the most part, women don't care about winning; they just want to be understood.*

Here's the craziest thing of all: For the most part, women don't care about winning; they just want to be understood. Men love competition and the feeling of winning, Lord knows, I'm supremely guilty of this very thing! But in a healthy relationship, communication is about "teaming" and not being the star quarterback. You can be the star quarterback with everything else, but not with her; she wants to be part of a team. Even if she views you as the spiritual, financial, or whatever type leader of the relationship or family, she can and will at the same time consider herself a coequal when it's just the two of you behind closed doors. You'll be well served and respected more if you work on listening more than thinking about what you're going to say when it's your turn to talk or waiting for the right moment to butt in so that you'll be heard and can exert your masculinity.

In the movie *Pirates of the Caribbean*, there's a scene where Jack Sparrow is talking to Captain Barbossa. He says, "If that ship be sunk properly, then its Captain should be sunk with it!" Basically, what he is saying is that for a ship to be properly sunk, the captain must go down with the ship. The man and the ship are honorable and deemed worthy when they go down together. Conversely, a ship that is sunk without its captain aboard isn't properly sunk; it is sunk in shame because its captain abandoned ship. The point is this: Don't abandon ship when the communication gets tough and she's talking 65 percent more than you and pouring out her emotions—regardless of what the topic is. If you like to "win," then heed this advice: If you're at a loss for words and listening is all you have left, then you're in the right place. No matter how rough the seas, when the storm finally blows over and she realizes that you've listened and have truly understood her words, not only is your ship never going to sink, hers isn't either. The calmness that follows will be worth it. I promise with all my heart!

Men, take what I'm about to say to heart. In a healthy dating relationship, your ship is your girl. She belongs to you. She's yours because she allows it. You can set sail with her, and she'll take you wherever you want to go. She will be sturdy through all of life's storms, but you have to be attentive and treat her right no matter what the weather is doing. Your lack of communication, lack of initiative, wrong approach, and shorthand style of communication is the equivalent of throwing yourself overboard onto a puny, little dingy while the love of your life, your treasure, your lifeline, sinks to the bottom of the abyss. Don't be a coward that abandons the ship. Keep your hands softly on the wheel and don't try to control the storm. You can't. You simply must stay aboard and be prepared to go down with the ship—if it must go down! It's manly. It's proper. It's how it should work. Smooth seas and sunny blue skies never made a skilled captain! Go be the X-Man she wants you to be, she needs you to be; and she's waiting for you to rise to the occasion. And when you do, you will be blessed even beyond what you deserve. Man up!

CHAPTER 13

Wonder Woman

This chapter is for my sisters from another mister! Before I begin, let me admit that writing this section is a challenge because, well, I'm a dude! I'm a simple guy, yet I still feel that at this point in my life with all my life's experiences that I can offer a valuable opinion on many things that make a wonderful woman.

I've been tremendously blessed to be raised by amazing God-serving parents. My dad, Bob, taught me business, indomitable spirit, how to work with the public, and how to be a "real" man in my life's walk. Above all else, he believed that to be successful you simply have to work hard and never give up. Love ya, Pop! My mom, Bonnie, a wonderful Christ-following woman, taught me everything else. She was the rock in our home. To say she went above and beyond the call of duty as a mom, wife, and servant to all people she encountered would be a profound understatement. I understand so much better now as an adult and father myself about who she was when I was growing up. While growing up, my dad can be aptly quoted as saying more times than I can count, "I made a living, and she made life worth living!" When I was young, my dad traveled quite a bit for work and was gone often. That left my sister and me home with our mom. She was a schoolteacher, directed school plays, church plays, music teacher, leader in the church; and her regular words of wisdom were always just what I needed when I needed them—which was daily! She was a loving and caring mom and wife and was never hotheaded or gossipy. She lived with purpose and intention in all she endeavored.

Let me paint this picture with even more clarity, lest you believe my mom was a simple housewife from the Midwest. My mom was highly educated, very independent, made her own money and her own way. She was never known as "Bob's wife." She stood on her own name and was highly respected by everyone that came in contact with her. She was handy with power tools, could build anything she set her mind to, was a master seamstress—and Lord have mercy, can that girl cook a Thanksgiving supper like it's nobody's business! She was by my side in everything I did while growing up. All the sports which I traveled for hundreds of miles from home, my doctor visits, my broken bones, my terrible teens, and my moments of bad conduct. She was certainly not a woman that waited for Dad to get home to warm my britches if I needed it. Oh yeah, she was a Wonder Woman in every meaning of the term!

I strongly feel that magazines, social media, contemporary music and society as a whole today have defined the wrong meaning of a woman's life and purpose. What do I mean? In short, today, to be a Wonder Woman, you have to be a man. More specifically, it is suggested everywhere you turn that to be a Wonder Woman you have to not only be a man, but also still be all things that encompass being a woman. I'm 100 percent on board with workplace equality and things of that nature. However, the "feminism" aspect of being a contemporary woman has skewed femininity to a point that, honestly, I'm not even sure it will ever retract. Sadly, I also feel that this is due in part to the fact that we are currently living in an age of "weak men." Quite frankly, women have had to step up more than they ever have in the history of civilization.

This book isn't about anthropology nor is it about political viewpoints whatsoever! It's about being an adult who's dating where all these aforementioned conditions exist for men and women alike, and it's more difficult than ever. If you want to observe the pressures put on women to be "like men," you need only to go to any social media platform and read to your heart's content the thousands upon thousands of quotes, quips, and memes. Comments like "If he can do it, I can do it" are abundant, and those statements are the "kind" versions. They get increasingly more inflammatory the more you consume. I won't go into unnecessary details on these examples. Hopefully, you know what I mean.

Ladies, as a man, let me apologize on behalf of all my brethren. We've let you down. I hope this book and others like it will help educate our men and return them to the ways that are right. By "right," I mean, the right way to live as a man in a healthy, committed, monogamous relationship, the leader of the family unit, spiritual leadership, and living our purpose as men. We're still here. We're still necessary. We can still "right" this ship back on the proper course, and it will take you, the Wonder Woman, to help us get back to where we should be.

In my observation, the number one complaint I've heard above any other is this: "Why do men just want to get in my pants and never want to commit?"

I have talked to, listened to, and interviewed more women about the specific topic of dating than I can count. In my observation, the number one complaint I've heard above any other is this: "Why do men just want to get in my pants and never want to commit?" In this chapter, I want to focus on what women can do to curve their dating endeavors in the right direction. If you have never heard it from your momma, let me introduce a simple statement: "Why should he buy the cow if the milk is free?" I know, what a horrible analogy, but I'm sure somewhere along your dating journey this quote has come up in conversation. You've either said it, heard it, or both. In the numerous battle of the sexes conversations I've had with both genders, I've observed that women are running from pain and men are running towards pleasure. What that means is that women don't want to put themselves in an emotionally hurtful relationship, and men are seeking sexual pleasure first, as a precursor to an actual relationship. Neither gender is wrong for what drives them; it's a matter of meeting in the middle. I should also point out that this is not an all-encompassing sentiment directed at everyone, so if this doesn't apply to you, male or female, then just understand—as I'm sure you already do—that this is an average of all dating adults, typically speaking. What's the commonly used phrase these days? "It's a thing!"

The Roller Coaster

I love using analogies when it comes to talking about dating situationships. The term "situationship" refers to a relationship that is undefined and/or uncommitted. I love riding roller coasters. When I was a kid—and now as an adult— I'm that guy that will ride the same roller coaster over and over again because I love the butterflies I get in my belly when I go down that first big hill: head-pounding twists, breathtaking upside-down loops with my legs just dangling in the air, and the abrupt stop at the end. Yes! Yes! Yes! I can't get enough of the thrill it gives me. That's what the act of sex and the pursuit of sex is like for a man. Put another way, men would prefer to avoid the long and winding line where you have to wait forever just to get on the coaster and then wait a whole minute just to climb to the top of the coaster's first hill before that awesome drop hits. Men enjoy the thrill of the ride! Conversely, women love the long line where they can hold hands, talk, and speculate about all things in the "situationship"; and that climb up the first coaster hill is just as heart thumping as the rest of the ride. Imagine, if you will, a piece of paper with the infamous bell-shaped curve that we all studied in high school math. Looks a lot like a roller coaster, doesn't it? Women are on the far left, the starting point of the upward curve. This is where women like to begin. Men like to start at the top with their hands straight up in the air, already screaming, heart pounding, and preparing their very soul for the thrilling downward plunge that's the whole purpose of the ride. In real life, you can't enjoy the thrill of the roller coaster without waiting in the line and taking the ever-slow crawl up to the top of the first hill. However, in dating, it's very easy to just begin at the top and get right down to the business of the super fun thrill ride. Here's the rub, ladies: If you allow that to happen, then all you'll get is what you've always gotten. Sure, it will be thrilling and rewarding in the moment. Then much like a real roller coaster, it'll be brief. The sudden stop at the end will thrust your heart right up against your dating roller coaster's safety bar that's holding you in. I'm by no means suggesting that it's the woman's responsibility to control sexual activity as if it's a manual transmission with several gears to be used at different RPMs. I'm humorously pointing out, using the aforementioned analogy, the differences between the genders. On the average, men will take the path of least resistance and will do so to the point of intentionally avoiding any unnecessary friction that doesn't get them to the top of the roller coaster so they can get to the part they like best. This is not the case in an actual healthy, committed, monogamous relationship. If you have found yourself in a "situationship" and not a relationship that you desire, then this section should help shed some light on the matter.

Ok girls, I want to give you a list of things I've identified as the Top 10 things that men are desperately seeking in their Wonder Woman. Just like in the men's "X-Men" chapter, this is *my* list of the things that I have compiled after hours upon hours of talking to men, reading, studying, and just "feeling" my way to derive this list. If you can use this list as a common-sense guide to identify your own qualities or maybe just work on a couple, then you'll hit a home run with Mr. Right.

What He Wants In His Wonder Woman

1. She is beautiful to my eye, and I am attracted to her from head to toe.

2. She's not perfect, but she's perfect for me.

3. She knows how to handle me without making me feel guilty.

4. She is affectionate, passionate, and responds to my advances.

5. She lets me "be the man" and "be a man."

6. She isn't catty, gossipy, contemptuous, or demeaning to me or others.

7. She has realistic expectations of me.

8. She has a heart of forgiveness and understanding.

9. She is proud to be on my arm wherever we go, and we have fun together.

10. She is supportive of my endeavors, encourages me, and respects me.

And because of all these things, I find her irresistible; and I vow to surrender my life for her, our family, and to support her and be faithful always!

A Wonder Woman is not only the ship in the relationship but she is the lighthouse too. A Wonder Woman is a man's light that keeps him off the rocky shores and is the headlights on his dream car that guides him through the darkest of times and the best of times as well. The business of being a desirable woman in today's dating scene doesn't have to be risky business, but it does come with risks. There's a delicate balance between being all he needs and also maintaining your dignity and feminine qualities that makes women special. They are not opposing forces like a tug of war; they complement each other. And what man doesn't like to be kept on his toes! Women can't stand a lazy and sloven man, and men feel the exact same way. I once had a discussion with a sixty-five-year-old woman who said to me, "That a good woman can lift up a 'not-as-good' man and help raise him." She also went on to say that the reverse, on the average, isn't as true; that is, "Even a good man will struggle to lift up a woman that's not at his level to begin with." She's right; it's not fair, and I don't like it. But it's the truth. So then, my proud, strong, and independent women, it's just as important to have your affairs in order before commingling your life's personal trials with a would-be relationship. It's not wise to count on a man to pull you where you want to go. Ever heard the term "gold digger?" The most common inference to this modern-day dating term is a woman that is pursuing a man's interest because of his wealth or income. Yup, it's a thing. And it happens at all socioeconomic levels. It's not something that only occurs with well-to-do men dating women half their age. I want to change the meaning of this ugly term. I want to reframe it in a positive way and have it illustrate a quality that uniquely belongs to women. Women are looking for a golden man, not a man's gold. A Wonder Woman will dig through a muddy, sloppy hole and will dig and dig and keep digging until they strike gold: that gold being a man's character that is the right gold for her.

What I'm about to say is true for men and women alike, but I will admit that in my numerous observations it's much harder for women. That is, if you're an adult female, a Wonder Woman looking for your X-Man, you'll have to roll your sleeves up, get your hands dirty, and you'll have to pan for gold; that is, you'll have to "pan" for that man before you hit your pot of gold! It will take time and it will be frustrating. You may even lose your heart along the way a time or two, but it will be worth it in the end.

Any woman can be a Wonder Woman! The DC Comics character *Wonder Woman* is without a doubt one of the most powerful, caring, and hardest-working superheroes. She pulls her weight, and in no way is she a secondary character in the Justice League! My mom was a Wonder Woman, and like the character she represents, she was beautiful, worked long, hard hours, stood for all that was good, and she was absolutely a hero. Not only to me but to countless people throughout her life. She never waited for someone to give her the title of a superhero; she just became one because she chose to be and knew it was her calling. My mom would very often say to me, "Bloom where you are planted." If you're a single gal seeking your forever mate in life, it all starts with simply blooming right where you are; and the rest will fall into place.

CHAPTER 14

Raw Chemistry

Perhaps you're thinking that the chapters in this book have felt a bit academic, as if maybe this world is full of undateable people that so desperately need this material. Not entirely, but we all have some undateable tendencies. And who doesn't want some good information to consider as they plow ahead? It might sound as though maybe the system is wrong, warped, or even that you have to follow some type of procedure or manual to pursue your dating life. And when you do that, it will magically lead to true love in a "real" relationship, or even marriage. Let me say this: "I get it!" Maybe you're right. Regardless, the point isn't to turn you into a dating superhero but to expand your thinking as you approach your dating endeavors.

On that note, there's one thing I'm hugely passionate about, and it's so very important: raw chemistry! I have been so blessed to have experienced true chemistry not once, but twice in my life. Conversely, like many reading this book, I've also been through the tumultuous experience of trying to force raw chemistry when there was simply none to be had. Ugh! That's the worst, isn't it?

My first experience of raw chemistry happened to me early in life. I was not only madly in love, but I had a true partner in crime, and we played together like the best of friends.

My second experience was much later in life, and like the first, it was amazing! We were full-grown adults with busy lives, but we loved spending as much time together as we could—and the passion was indescribable! In both instances, there was no procedure to how we met or hit it off; it just seemed to flow organically. In the second instance, I must fully admit, the chemistry was instant from the very moment we met. We were head over heels for each other, and neither of us could explain how or why. It was like winning the lottery, except it was better than any amount of money. It was pure magic!

Raw chemistry can be wonderful, and it can be a three-headed dragon that's nearly impossible to slay. If it's with the right person, it's like a dream come true. If it's with the wrong person, it's so blinding that you can lose your immortal soul!

I'm truly a believer in the law of attraction, but raw chemistry is a different animal. Most would say it's either there or it isn't. I get that, but I don't 100 percent agree. I think the world can provide many examples of very happy couples in long-term relationships that didn't start out with strong raw chemistry. Raw chemistry can be wonderful, and it can be a three-headed dragon that's nearly impossible to slay. If it's with the right person, it's like a dream come true. If it's with the wrong person, it's so blinding that you can lose your immortal soul!

Let me be clear about what I mean when I say "raw chemistry" and what it means versus what most people think it means. In its most simplistic form, raw chemistry can be defined as an overwhelming and undeniable romantic attraction and sexual tension that can make your heart skip a beat. It is the equivalent of catnip—for humans! It'll make you feel and behave like a crazy person that says and does things they can't believe they're doing. If you're in a long-term relationship and you have that type of raw chemistry, then please immediately submit yourself and your significant other for dissection, study, and years of scientific research. Then the rest of us can learn from it and, with any luck, can figure out how to bottle it and sell it for absurd amounts of money. But if you're one of the majority that has yet to find it or figure it out, read on!

Whether you're a young adult, middle aged, or a senior, you probably already intuitively know that raw chemistry dilutes as you get older. It doesn't disappear, by any means; it just gets muted by your past experiences from dating, long-term relationships, or even past marriages that ended in divorce, or worse, the death of a loved one. I want to be clear about one thing, though: It doesn't matter what age you are or your gender; you are fully enabled and designed to experience raw chemistry. It lives in you, and it drives your everyday decisions. Yes, even your experiences outside of romantic inclinations are powered by your need to seek and experience raw chemistry in all you do.

My dad taught me from a very early age in the business and entrepreneurial world that the things that come easy, naturally— and almost seem to fall in your lap— are what's best for you and make the most money. He was right, as he has been many times in my life, advising me on all matters throughout my adulthood.

I like to call this "mojo." Like the law of attraction, your mojo is your headlight in life. No matter what direction you steer, that headlight is allowing you to see what's right in front of you and in the distance. It sends signals to your brain that let you know if you should stay on that seemingly "right track" or if you should change directions. However, unlike the business world, that same mojo can keep you on a track that, before you know it, you're stalled and going nowhere—only to have a 100-ton train hit you right in the driver's side door and render your emotions lifeless and broken.

Perhaps that very thing has happened to you even recently, and that's what led you to pick up this book in the first place. The very thing (your mojo) that serves you so well in your work and extracurricular activities can also be your nemesis when it comes to navigating dating and relationships, thus leaving you feeling increasingly undateable with every relationship that passes. Admit it, this is you. You've been here! Lord knows this is a vicious cycle I've been through. So much so I was compelled to write a book. The only way you can solve this is by being honest with yourself about it. Women try too hard, and men don't try hard enough. On average, women work too hard on their dating "project," and men are too quick to just kick it to the curb if it doesn't feel right within a few dates or a few months.

So how do we solve this all-too-familiar undateable dilemma? Better yet, is it something that even needs to be solved? I believe the latter; that is, it's not a dilemma, and your mojo isn't broken, but rather this is an exercise that you work on through self-analysis and practice. To be even more crystal clear, if you do happen to experience that all-desirable mutual raw chemistry experience, don't run from it but embrace it and hold on to it. It's worth it. Don't let it cripple you or mislead you into believing that something meaningful exists when in actuality the hot sex and great times you're having don't always translate into long-term relationship material. Enjoy it while it lasts and listen to your subconscious when it's telling you that this fling has an expiration date. I know what you're thinking about my writing right now: *This guy is all over the place and is talking out of both sides of his mouth.* Well, my friends, that is what's so crazy about raw chemistry: It feels so hot and cold sometimes, and it seems there is never a happy medium. That's how this thing works. It can be confusing and impulsive. But rest assured, your mojo is a living entity in your body, and you should work harder to amplify its power rather than quash it because of your past experiences.

This book and many like it preach to you about the procedures and protocols of what to do and what not to do on your self-imposed self-help journey to improve whatever aspect of your life you're working toward. But at the end of the day, you have to place your trust in your God-given mojo instincts and trust your headlights—just like a commercial airline pilot trusts their hundreds of instruments in the cockpit. Dating without trusting your mojo is like trying to land an airplane without any direction from the instrument panel. Get back to the basics!

Remember when you were younger and before you were working so many hours, paying bills, and battling the complexities of life, like raising kids, worrying about having kids because time is running out, listening to everyone's opinion about everything, and all that crap? Remember the time you were at summer camp and you met that guy from another state? You knew that whatever was going to happen, it was going to happen in that one week. And whatever happened, you were okay with it because you were insanely infatuated. You just couldn't wait to see him at the rec hall, or the pool, or during chapel. Your mojo was glowing like a new sunrise, and you could feel the same from him. That's what I mean by getting back to the basics. The only thing that makes it complicated is *you*. Stop making it complicated for yourself. Seriously, get the dark clouds out of your head and invite the sunshine back into your dating life again.

<hr />

Ms. Summertime-Sunshine-Fun Time!

There was a time in my life that I loved to go bowling, and a new bowling alley had just opened up nearby. On opening night, I gleefully went inside with my shiny ball and shoes, and I was ready to strut! If knocking down pins was a sin, I was surely going to hell! I loved bowling like a kid loves getting that perfect toy when opening their McDonald's Happy Meal—the lights, the sounds, the greasy food, the clashing of pins and, most of all, the competition. By the way, I suck at bowling, but I love the sport and the atmosphere.

I was on cloud nine after my first set, and I was ready for a stiff drink. I swaggered up to the food counter, and there she was—and I mean my face must have looked like some ugly dog meme on social media. My ears were perked up, my tongue was half hanging out, and I might as well have just proposed at first sight. She had that perfect body type that I liked, complete with blonde hair and a super sassy personality—the queen of sarcasm and tons of bowling lingo that only an experienced bowler knows.

Now, let me get one thing straight: Nothing happened. In fact, nothing happened for years. Not even any flirting! For ten years I bowled there and never even knew her last name or anything about her. We weren't even friends on social media. Nothing happened because we were both happily married and just going about our normal life. But the instant raw chemistry between us was absolutely undeniable. I'll insert this now rather than later: After all those years, and when we did eventually start dating, I asked her, "Was it just me or did you feel it, too, all those years ago?" She immediately responded with, "I was going to ask you the same question." Enough said. The raw chemistry between us was out of this galaxy, and our dating commenced.

We dated for an extremely mutually gratifying two and a half months, and then it ended. We never committed to a boyfriend/ girlfriend relationship; we just existed in each other's world as often as we could. Every time we got together was better than the time before, but I knew that while this terrific gal was an absolute blast, she just wasn't my soul mate. Ugh! It crushed her when I told her, and rightfully so. Pissed would be a better word. Nevertheless, I was honest about how I felt when I told her I wanted to begin seeing someone else that I had recently met. We didn't speak for, oddly enough, two and a half months, and then we made a truce. The bottom line was that our relationship was developing into more than just a summer fling and wasn't what I wanted; and it turns out that in the end we made much better friends than we did anything else. The "situationship" morphed into a friendship, and it was great!

The moral to this story—and the one or more personal stories of your own you're thinking about right now—is that just because you experience unbridled raw chemistry and get along great when you're together, if you know it's not a long-term relationship, then you should speak up and get on the same page with that person. Sometimes you'll find that they were thinking the same thing; other times you'll find that they were thinking it was blossoming into something much more. In either case, communicating or "checking in" on a regular basis is a good idea in order to avoid ruining your own reputation, or worse, losing a great life-long friend.

Regardless of what someone's moral or faith position is, most all adults, when being honest, admit that they've had a relationship(s) that they just can't help but continue having unbridled sex, frivolous dating, and whatever happens, happens. The truth is, the majority of these "situationships" do not end well and can cause further emotional damage that leads to an undateable mindset. It just gets worse every time as resentment, confusion, and numbness dig into your soul.

Listening to your mojo instincts does not mean you have to submit to them. Giving in to versus understanding your mojo are two very different things. Only you can navigate yourself in the right direction, and only you can allow yourself to get blindsided by the 100-ton train when you thought you were on the right track, but in fact, you were stalling like a sitting duck just waiting to be shot in the head.

I have spent so, so many years learning to channel my mojo into my work ethic, my personal health and fitness, and my faith walk. In all those cases, I have veered on and off the right track; but as I've aged, I've taught myself how to stay on the right track more often than not. The thing about getting hit by a train a few times is that you tend to learn from it. Is it time for you to learn what you already know? Is it time to get back to the basics, the simplicity of how your mojo works and when you seek and find that internal raw chemistry in another person? Are you wise and experienced enough now to differentiate between what is a fling versus what is genuine care and passion to stay with that person no matter what? Ponder this: If that one or two—or maybe three—things that other person does (or did) that makes your mojo spike to new levels were to suddenly pause or maybe even end due to injury, health problems, financial misfortune, relocation, or whatever, would they still be your best friend for life? Would they still ignite your mojo in other ways? Would you be able to sustain, even if only at a lower level, your mojo for them? If that significant other were to ponder these same questions, would they answer the same? If the answer is "Yes," then toot your train whistle and move full steam ahead! If not, then you need to consider having a serious come-to-Jesus meeting with yourself followed by some serious communication with that other person, and be prepared for possibly an abrupt dismissal of your future together.

Getting back to the basics of understanding that your mojo is simple but not easy. What's simple about it is that humans have a profound emotional memory. It's just one of many things that separates us from the animal kingdom. It's a simple exercise to compare your relationships and how your mojo played a role in your romantic endeavors in your teens versus your twenties and each decade thereafter. When you were young, your mojo was like an unbroken horse. It was wild and carefree, and you could roam anywhere you wanted. As you got older, you learned what to avoid because you knew it wasn't good for you or you knew it led nowhere. The unfortunate product of all of these learning experiences is that while you've gotten wiser, you have also built a new wall of boulders between you and the person that could have been, or will be, that one person that will walk into your life and is prepared to walk life with you no matter what. Those walls created your undateable mindset. It's the open wounds you still carry each and every day that you've not healed from or that you're still angry about that are dimming your headlights to the point you've just run off into the ditch and you don't even care. And, by God, you're just going to give up altogether and stay in the hole that you alone are responsible for getting yourself out of. I know you feel me right now! You have a powerful emotional memory, and you will return to your youthful mojo if you're committed to doing so. Yes, this is a mindset, but it's so much more. It's a process, and it's something you'll have to grow through on this journey over the coming weeks and months. Open yourself to being vulnerable again and, for heaven's sake, to being fun, spontaneous, and energized again. And do it with the intention of meeting your soul mate. If you're not in the market for a soul mate, that's fine too. How about just having a simple, slow relationship with a great man or woman whom you can share your next few weekends with or just coffee once a week.

Start with a friendship in mind, a real in-person friendship and not a social media or dating app late-night pen pal. If that person's headlights veer them off in another direction, then that's fine, you don't have to be hurt from it; just keep up the search. Notice I didn't say to keep up the good fight—this is not a fight or a struggle. You're not in survival mode; you're in thrive mode. Stay on that course! Channeling your mojo properly means that this will happen easily and naturally. Your mojo is a light that glows from the inside out. You're looking for a twin flame that burns how you burn and is at your level. If you make that your mindset, then I can assure you that is what you'll start attracting. A word of caution here: This book isn't about whether or not to engage sexually. But know this, if you do—and it's too soon—your mojo can and likely will morph into that three-headed dragon I spoke about earlier.

A raw chemistry attraction and interaction is like starting a small business: Start small, let it grow naturally, and don't hurry it. Investing tons of money and time will have very little long-lasting effect compared to patience and persistence.

Raw chemistry is real, and it is the most powerful force in my life. It can turn on you in the blink of an eye if you let go of the reins. It's a life force that can build your best life ever, and it can also burn you to the ground. Insert the emphasis and often-tattooed image of the "phoenix" cliche here. Yes, you can resurrect yourself using the principles in this book and recognize that you're vulnerable when you share your body with another person and the two of you are not on the same page. A raw chemistry attraction and interaction is like starting a small business: Start small, let it grow naturally, and don't hurry it. Investing tons of money and time will have very little long-lasting effect compared to patience and persistence.

In this chapter, I wanted to dispel the notion of fairy-tale endings, as they're fiction, not a fact of life. Instead, I'll leave you with this: As my friend Spok would say with his split-finger hand gesture in the air, "Go forth and prosper."

Now that's a guy that had mojo!

CHAPTER 15

To Love Again: That is the Question

If there were any chapter in this book that I could turn into a book of its own, it's this one. To love again: That is the question. I can liken the experience of that moment when you realize you're in love to be nothing short of spiritual. One of the dilemmas associated with being undateable is that you've envisioned the process of falling in love to be much like that of rendering animal fat to make bar soap. It takes a sacrifice, lots of hard work, boiling heat, and then finally a mold to give it the shape it ultimately becomes. Total hogwash! That's old-school soapmaking, and that's also old-school thinking when it comes to the formation of a healthy relationship.

Thus far in this book, we've set the stage of converting yourself from an undateable person into someone who is dateable and self-confident. So what do you do when you've readied yourself for the ultimate dating experience and you're headed out to sea for the fishing expedition of a lifetime? You've been on a few dates, and you've come across that seemingly Mr. or Ms. Right. Now what? What's next? Do we just keep dating and let it all flow naturally and see how it goes? What's the right amount of time? Who says those all-powerful three little words first? What's the checklist for that all-mighty-love connection?

A quick internet search suggests that for men it takes an average of 88 days to say "I love you," and, for women, 134.

A quick internet search suggests that for men it takes an average of 88 days to say "I love you," and, for women, 134. Yet with a lot of couples I know—and even with my own experiences—I've found that these averages can vary widely. Pause for a moment and think about all the people you know, what their love story is, how it developed, and over what period of time. I think you, too, will find that no love story is the same as another. The truth is that there is no one mold that neither I nor anyone can really recommend that's tried and true every time. You can do all the self-improvement in the world, ready yourself and set your standards (and stick to them), yet what you'll find is that it just takes time and patience. I do, however, want to offer you a couple of enlightened suggestions to track your progress on this journey.

First, I want to suggest that once you've entered into a committed and monogamous relationship, that one year is a good marker as far as knowing if you "know" this person and they "know" you and that your relationship is worth keeping and continuing to work on. Why one year? Several reasons! In the span of a year, you've had enough time together to fully encounter the other person's world and all it encompasses; and they've had the same experience with you. In that one year, you've heard all their stories about work, family, friendships, hardships, heartbreaks, and more. You've also been through all the seasons of the year, every holiday, and likely, a few family gatherings. You've not only heard about their world outside of dating you, you've also been introduced to it and been a part of many of the things in their world—the things they had going on day-to-day, week-to-week, and month-to-month that were in place before you were in the picture. The same is true in reverse: They know your world too. All those mutual and combined experiences are your clues as to whether or not your relationship has what it takes to go the distance. If you're still not sure, then hopefully you've been an active partner in the relationship and there has been ample communication around what you're thinking and feeling. Even then, it doesn't mean you should exit stage left; it simply means that more time could be needed. But if you know it's not going to work, then "to thine own self be true," and perhaps it's time to get to the conclusion.

In my experience, one thing I have found to be true every single time is that (1) two people feel exactly the same way, or (2) they feel the exact opposite, and one is likely head over heels; the other, well, not so much. Either way—and as suggested numerous times in this book—a healthy relationship is comfortable with a periodic "check in" on things to ensure you're both on the same page. If the two of you feel the same way, then full steam ahead. If you're thinking in the back of your mind that your partner isn't on the same page with you, then it's definitely time to have a "come-to-Jesus" meeting with yourself first and your partner second. If the latter is true, then it's likely also true that the time to communicate your concern is past due, and perhaps the other person is waiting for you to initiate the conversation. Not talking about the big, white elephant in the room isn't healthy, so get to it.

Falling in love the right way is a lot like fishing. You can have the best equipment, the right experiences, the best map, or even someone to guide you, yet you can get to the right spot at the right time, and on that particular day, the fish just weren't biting, and you go home empty-handed. It happens in fishing, and it happens in all love pursuits. Just because this particular relationship ended empty-handed, it doesn't mean you were wrong, the other person was wrong, or even that something went wrong; it simply means that it just wasn't a match. Recognize that it happens. Whether it's 88 days, 134 days, or 365 days, it's best to keep checking in with yourself and your partner too. All things in life change, and change is good. It keeps us moving forward and looking upward.

Don't fear the change in a relationship's status from one month to another. Like all things in life, change is a constant and should be expected. An ending to one relationship isn't a failure on yours or the other person's part. It's a new beginning, and this time with more information and experience to improve the next one.

Second, I feel deeply to the core of my body that a vital missing element to today's dating experiences and relationships is the spiritual nature of the human soul. I don't want to get deeply scientific anymore than I want to get deeply religious, but when you were delivered into this world you were a human with a soul, and that's all you were. As you grew older, and with every life experience, you developed into the person you are today. You have a soul that lives in you, and no matter how faint it may seem to you at different times, even right now, your soul is alive and well; its light never diminishes. You've allowed yourself to mute it at different times in your life for a myriad of reasons, but now is the time to awaken that inner being that is your soul and allow someone else to carry your light with you—when the time is right.

So what does it feel like to release and respond to your own soul in the context of dating? The Holy Bible reads in 1 Corinthians 13:4–7: "Love is patient, love is kind. It does not envy, it does not boast, it is not proud. It does not dishonor others, it is not self-seeking, it is not easily angered, it keeps no record of wrongs. Love does not delight in evil but rejoices with the truth. It always protects, always trusts, always hopes, always perseveres." It is in this brief text that I feel true love is manifested in the context of letting your inner light, your soul, shine outwardly from you and into the hands of the person you love. When you read this biblical verse often quoted by a minister during a wedding, does it speak to you about your past—or even current—relationship(s); or perhaps it gives you some direction for the future? If you're truly being honest with yourself, the answer is "Yes."

The amazing thing about this often-quoted biblical text is that it was written over two thousand years ago, yet it is still applicable today. The problem, as I alluded to in the opening pages, is that we've become such autonomous single creatures—married people too—that seem to be more focused on watching life's guardrails rather than keeping our eyes on the road. Do you remember from your driver's education class that the instructor would say, "Even experienced drivers tend to steer in the direction of what they're looking at?" What that means is stop looking in your rearview mirror while trying to move forward. It means stop looking at the guardrail the whole time and keep your eyes on the road. Looking at your rearview mirror or at the guardrail while you're driving through your dating experience is one of the things that *was* making you undateable. Put your blinders on, drive straight, and do it with intention. If your soul is speaking the words from Corinthians, then you're in the right place to give and to receive true love. If not, then you're not quite there yet.

Reading this book is a step in the right direction. Doing the hard work to make personal investments in yourself through reading, study, prayer, counseling, and to improve your self-awareness, self-confidence—all to alert you to your own flaws—is tremendous forward movement. Remember, motion creates opportunity; and it does so in all facets of your life, not just in your dating.

Ms. Resentment

I met her online, and we hit it off right away. She was smart, wickedly funny, and oh, was she gorgeous. Honestly, everything about her was perfect from head to toe and from the inside to the outside. She had some serious life trials; and through it all, she always came out on top and was surviving life in all aspects: positive attitude, single mom, career woman, physically fit—and she was very successful at all four.

We dated for awhile, and it became the right type of serious relationship each and every week. We communicated well, and we didn't hold back on tough topics. When we went on dates, both of us truly left our worlds behind for those few hours. It was like we were high school kids just living for the moment and living with the simple joy we found in each other. It was a match made in heaven. One month we hit a snag, and it seemed to snowball no matter how hard we loved each other and worked to fix and re-create our former harmonious existence. She sent a text to my friend expressing her concern about me. The text was very detailed and didn't put me or the situation in its full light. I could tell instantly that she wrote the text in such a way to elevate my friend's perception about how wonderful she was and how perfect she was for me, but that I wasn't living up to her standards. My friend actually copy/pasted the whole text to me so I could read it. I never said anything to the girl I was dating because I didn't want to inflame the situation nor create any awkwardness between her and my friend. I chose instead to take it on the chin by simply telling my friend the whole story and just letting it go, chalking it up to an isolated event.

Earlier in our relationship, we agreed that we could ask the other for their smartphone to observe or read anything. During this time, on several occasions she asked me for my phone, and I always happily handed it to her. She would sit on the couch and spend ten to fifteen minutes going through anything she wanted and ask me any questions she wanted to. I would answer, and then it was over. Honestly, I never minded because I kept my nose clean, and I also knew this had more to do with her past relationship traumas than it did with me. It's how she made herself comfortable with us and with me. It is what it is, and I just rolled with it with no disputes or so much as rolling my eyes. In all that time, I never once asked to see her phone. Yes, I wanted to, but I chose to just trust, have faith, and set an example rather than perpetuating the behavior. I wanted her to figure out that this hot topic was centric to her and not to me.

It wasn't long after she sent that text to my friend that she asked to see my phone. I had deleted the text from my friend because in my gut I knew it was coming; that is, that she was going to ask to see my phone and check on whether my friend and I had talked about it—and, of course, to see what else perhaps was going on in my world. I know how all that looks, but that is truly the only time I've ever done that. I handed her my phone, and for the first time, I asked to see hers in return. The look on her face was utter shock! I had never asked to see her phone before. Her look of shock turned to a ghost-white face as she said nothing and handed it to me. She sat down, as did I, across the room from each other. She went through my phone for a few minutes and said she was done. I went through her phone for a solid forty-five minutes and never said a word. What I found on her phone were text messages between some past boyfriends and her. To be honest, I didn't see anything that I felt was a relationship-ending incident. I certainly raised an eyebrow at a few things but nothing that I felt was totally out of line. What I did find was an extensive and months-long dialogue between her and one of her family members that, once again, did not put me in a good light. I understand that people will seek counsel from their other close family members, but the things she said about me (and her family member's responses) were utterly disgusting. I was floored! She sat there the whole time staring at me while I switched apps and scrolled while reading and rereading. I could tell she was getting very agitated. I even found a password-protected picture vault app. I did ask her about that, and her response was—I felt at the time—honest. She said it was pictures of her and her past boyfriends and that she didn't even look at it. I didn't ask her for the secret pin to unlock the app. Instead, I waited to see if she would offer it because I asked about it. She didn't. I moved on, thinking that perhaps it was best I didn't see what all was in there. I just wanted to trust her and not give her a reason to resent me for demanding entry into the app. Plus, she and I had many pictures together, and I knew that while most of those pictures were just innocent, fun pictures, there certainly were some that I wouldn't want the outside world to see. I assumed that what was in her secret vault app were images that were best not seen by me. I didn't need those images in my head. What's in the past is in the past. At the end of that exhausting exercise, we had a healthy fight that kept getting worse and worse that led to her eventually leaving my life forever weeks later.

The moral of that sad story is that regardless of how great a couple we were on the surface, underneath our seemingly perfect love for each other was a lot of mistrust, contempt, and massive unresolved past resentments on her part. Basically, our relationship was the exact opposite of 1 Corinthians 13:4–7. It was as if our entire relationship was the word-for-word opposite of everything stated in the aforementioned bible verse.

To address the question whether to love again, the answer is yes. Y-E-S! Because you were born to become an ever-increasing self-aware spiritual creature, you are designed and purposed for love. It doesn't mean to be reckless anymore than it does freewheeling. It means don't be afraid to swallow the red pill rather than floating through life's falsities offered by the blue pill. Know that if you are designed for love, then you are also capable of receiving it and giving it equally. You deserve it; and anything that you are purposed for you must also work for. By "work for," I mean working on yourself more than working on a relationship.

Has there ever been a greater genius on this planet than Albert Einstein? Has there ever been a better advocate for peace and servitude than Mother Theresa? Has there ever been a better brand ambassador than Michael Jordan? Most likely, the answer is yes. The difference is, those aforementioned people and countless others like them in their areas of notoriety did so because they knew their blessings and their gifts were only worth as much as the work they were willing to put into them. You have to do the work on yourself and have patience. It will pay off. I promise! If you're staring at the rearview mirror calculating your past mistakes and adding up how this current relationship is going to be the same—or staring at the guardrail so much that you can see the sparks flying—then be smart; take your foot off the gas and tap the brake. The only head-on collision that will happen from this point forward will be the one you yourself cause.

But wait, there's more to this: A massive problem with moving on and chasing love one more time is that we often try to recreate the best parts of our past relationship(s). To be more specific, what I mean is that we date with the unconscious intention of finding that person that reminds us of our long-lost and/or last love. We attempt to resurrect that person that made us feel the happiest in a previous relationship, in our current relationship. I am sad to say that I am an expert at doing this myself, and the end result, unfortunately, is the same; it doesn't work. In fact, the degree to which it doesn't work is even worse than the time it didn't work out with the other person. That's not a profound notion, but when I came to the realization that I myself was doing it, it hit me like a ton of bricks. Ugh! Why am I doing this to myself? What's even worse, what am I doing to the other person who's most likely completely oblivious? Your previous wonderful and perfect relationship that didn't work out for whatever reason is akin to the sinking of the *Titanic*. Yes, in its day, it was a beautiful and elaborate ship that offered all the world's finest emotions, touches, and tingles. But why in the hell would you try to raise that ship from Davy Jones's locker? Listen, that ship has sunk! Taking the time to raise that previous version of a relationship from the dead, trying to clean it off and make it look as shiny as it was before is an enormous and wasteful emotional investment. What do you think will cost you more emotional currency, resurrecting that old sunken ship or just building a new one from scratch? The answer is obvious—at least I hope it is. That past relationship had its chance. It didn't work. Leave it on the bottom of the ocean where it belongs!

The movie *Multiplicity* came out in 1996 and featured Michel Keaton. In that movie, Keaton figures out a way to clone himself so that he has more time to get things done, including spending more time with his wife. Each time he made a clone of himself, that carbon copy got more and more wacky and progressively less like himself. Like the movie, if you're attempting to clone your past relationship(s), it's going to get out of hand—and not only end just like the last one, but you'll cause yourself increasing and unnecessary damage. Start fresh. Start new. Have a new outlook and an open mind. Your seemingly perfect past relationship had its own fingerprint, and it's unique to just you and that last person. You can't body snatch that other relationship's fingerprint and expect a happy ending in a new relationship. As my daddy would say, "It just doesn't work like that!"

CHAPTER 16

Graduate From Undateable to Dateable

You've made it. How do you feel? I hope that your reading or listening to this book was as insightful and helpful to you as it was for me during the process of writing it. There are so many "morals to the story" as you read the pages of this book, but the ultimate impact I hope to have on your life—as it has had on my life—is this: to move from your current mindset of being undateable to your new mindset of being awesomely dateable. What do I mean? There is one primary reason why a person is undateable: It is because you have a tremendous amount of personal work to do on your soul, your body, and your mindset. Once you've done the work, you will become dateable and be ready to experience—perhaps for the first time ever—a truly loving, caring, giving, honest, and 100 percent monogamous relationship with the person of your dreams.

For me, as a single person, I long to graduate to a new and refreshed dateable mindset so that I can finally be in a relationship with my co-equal, that incredibly unique person that's exactly what I want and need to share my life with and that I don't even think about being with anyone else—past, present, or future. Just her! Like you, I know going into this that it takes a ton of personal work. And only when that is done can I truly be the awesome man of another woman's dreams and I will be fully deserving of her.

Some call it a secret. Some call it a mystery of the universe. Some call it blindly obvious. Some will even say it's impossible. I say it's all of these. That is, for some crazy reason, the moment you accept that you need to give up looking and trying so hard and instead simply exist and focus on yourself is when the right person seems to drop into your life out of absolutely thin air. This has not happened to me—yet! But I can feel myself being more ready and more deserving every day that goes by. I can tell that my mind is bending to God's will for me and the universe is letting me know each and every day that I'm getting closer. But I'm just not quite ready yet. I will hold steady. I will fast the desires of my heart. I will wait! While I am waiting, I will mediate, pray, work on myself, educate, and prepare for that one person that is perhaps even genetically designed by God to be my forever soulmate. I will pray the undateable prayer:

Hello, God, it's me again. I am struggling with my loneliness and my desire to be in a healthy, committed relationship. Please give me peace and comfort and teach me patience. Be with me in my time of solitude and show me your presence and your timing for all things. Allow me to use this solitary time to grow personally, professionally, financially, and closer to you. Ordain me with the wisdom to accept that whether you have the ultimate person for me or not, that your will and your presence will live in me and shine out of me. I love my life, God, and I long for the right person to spend it with. Please, God, send me the right person and give me the wisdom to recognize it and the time it needs to grow with your blessing. Thank you, God, for your many blessings on my life, and be with me always. Keep me safe, healthy, and continue to work in me and through me to bless others. God, please be with me in my moments of contempt, anger, resentment, and utter sin. I am a constant work in progress, and with you in my life I know I cannot fail, and your blessings will pour down on me always. Amen!

Whether you believe in the Almighty or not, this prayer is powerful and can be made into meditation or suited to whatever your faith walk is. As you're reading this very section right now, know that I am praying and thinking of you. Right now, millions of people walk this earth that are exactly where you are right now; and there are just as many people through all the ages of mankind that did the work and got to their victory with that one special and forever soulmate. It was not luck! It was not fate! It was not sheer will! It was days, months, and even years of work both before and during their dating journey to find their soul-mate. This is what successful relationships do. They endure this so they can say they are happily in love and that the person they chose to spend their life with is absolutely the single-most important and right decision they've ever made in their life. You are worthy of this. You deserve this. You can have this too.

A favorite quote of mine is something that my mom instilled in me from a very young age. Gently she would say, "If it is to be, it is up to me." So true!

CHAPTER 17

Dating for Married Couples

Whether you've been married for one year or more than fifty, the importance of dating doesn't diminish. In fact, it becomes even more important. For whatever reason, it is common in marriages that once the honeymoon is over, all the romance of premarriage dating seems to taper off. This happens for many reasons both good and bad. Having been previously married twice, totalling nearly twenty years, I really gave this some thought as to why it happens and what married couples can do about it.

> *Trust me; intentional dating in a marriage will stave off a ton of problems before they ever have a chance to begin.*

First things first: Ask yourself if you and your spouse date like you used to before you were married. Chances are your answer is no. The reason is varied, but on the average, the reason as to why it happens boils down to one thing: availability. Previously in this book, I really drove home the point that to move from being undateable to dateable you have to be available for dating. That is, do you, or are you making time to date in the first place? In marriage, the problem is quite the opposite: Couples spend so much time together simply living their lives that the notion of dating is often absent. Couples might say, "Why do we need to date? We see each other every day." Others might say, "We don't have to date anymore. I've got him, he's got me, and we love our life." All of that makes perfect sense, and it isn't necessarily wrong. But what happens is a couple starts to live *in* their life rather than *living* their life together as a loving, caring, and passionate team. This dilemma gets compounded exponentially when you add children to the mix, increased work demands, and a laundry list of other things. Dad coaches the kid's sports team, Mom does the PTO (parent-teacher organization), and they both work long hours. By Friday night, all they want to do is just relax, ya know, watch Netflix and Chill. When this status quo sets in and becomes a habit, it's just a matter of time before the marriage becomes more like a business partnership with your co-parenting roommate, and out of nowhere, marriage issues develop. This dilemma is a plague on a marriage equivalent to drowning your marriage's soul with one drop of water at a time. Like a locomotive leaving the train station, it moves too slow to notice, but once it gathers speed, it's moving too fast to stop. Trust me; intentional dating in a marriage will stave off a ton of problems before they ever have a chance to begin.

The point of continuing to date when you're married, just like when you were formally courting, is to make time for face to face communication. If you've made it this far in this book, then you already know that a key component of a healthy and romantic relationship is simple conversation—like what you did before you were married. The solution appears to be simple; but as with all things "simple," they're not always "easy" to accomplish. I think it's important to establish some ground rules for dating while you're married to ensure that the date itself is healthy and truly keeps the spark alive.

Here is a list of do's and don'ts when dating your spouse:

1. If you didn't do it when you were courting prior to marriage, then don't do it now. Treat the date with your spouse like it's the first, second, or third date you went on before you got married. Remember the magic!

2. Don't rush him/her and persist on asking if they're ready to go yet. Ladies, get dolled up like you used to. Men, shave your face, wear a sexy shirt, and be a perfect gentleman.

3. Going on a "couples date" with another married couple or group of married couples does not constitute a date between you and your spouse if that's all the dating you do. A real date is one-on-one with your spouse.

4. Leave your mobile phones/devices in the car. The one exception might be if you're leaving a young child at home with a babysitter and you just have to keep your phone on you. If you're in the middle of a "big deal" at work or "on call," then you should wait for a night that those aren't the terms of the date prior to going out.

5. Netflix and Chill is a great date night, but it isn't the be-all and end-all solution to dating for married couples. A real date is when two people leave their home, meet up, walk, hold hands, compliment each other, have a drink, eat a meal, and/ or sit together and talk. Netflix and Chill is something you

do after the date.

6. Don't talk about things on the date that you can talk about at home. If your youngest is potty training, that's not a great date-night topic. Also, you can certainly do some chitchat about work stuff, but it can't be the whole conversation. C'mon now, you two love each other; talk about that instead. Talk about a vacation with just the two of you. Talk about your dreams and what feeds your life's desires, not how long it's been since the car was last detailed or how little Susie's grades could be better.

7. Don't talk about other couple's relationship problems. This seems like a no-brainer, but it's an easy conversational trap to fall into. Abort Mission! Avoid this topic like the plague!

8. Go to different places other than your usual hangout. Hiking. Biking. Walking a trail. The park. Hockey game. Go see Christmas lights. Hell, make love in the backseat. Go for it! (not in your kid's school parking lot) Dating your spouse should be as spontaneous and adventurous as it was when you first met.

9. If dating in your marriage is a new thing you and your spouse are trying out, don't overdo it, especially if this is a response to an already-hurting marriage relationship. Don't feel like you've got to shock the marriage with sudden romantic intentions. Keep it light. Keep it easy. Just enjoy the moment no matter what you're doing. Dating won't cure a marriage's issues, but it most certainly can be a positive experience between both people that breeds hope, renewed love, and optimism for the future.

The upcoming date night doesn't have to wait for the actual night to begin. A few days before the date send text messages to her to let her know how excited you are to pick her up in the driveway. Ladies, pick up a new outfit he hasn't seen you in before, or a new lipstick color—and wear it for the first time on date night.

Remember, when dating your spouse, the point is so that you can refresh your connection outside of your day to day life. I purposely used the word "refresh" because it should be an experience that is the opposite of stagnation. I've lost count of how many times I've heard a couple say, "Yeah, we haven't been out together in years." Don't let that become your marriage. And if that describes it, it's never too late to start your refresher course on dating the love of your life. Believe me, she'll love and adore you so much more for the effort. Men, I'm an old-fashioned kinda dude, so for you, this is your opportunity to reestablish that you are "the man" in the relationship; and as such, you are designed to chase what you want. And she so wants to be desired and chased by you. Do not ask your bride if she wants to go out sometime in the next month or so. Instead, if you want to be "terrific," you have to be "specific." Plan the date. Set the day and time. Go to her and say, "Hey babe, I planned a date night for just the two of us. Can I pick you up this Friday at 7:00 p.m. and take you on a fun date night?" I don't care if your wife is a hardened CEO of the largest multinational corporation in the world—get a mop, fellas, 'cause she's about to melt right in front of you. If you want greatness in your marriage, then be the first to give it. Men, in this author's opinion, it's your job to initiate. Just do it!

I remember many years ago I was blessed with the opportunity to meet Dr. Gary Chapman, author of *The Five Love Languages*, in person at a church in St. Louis. I attended a seminar he was hosting. During this event, I remember something he said that resonated with me like nothing ever had before in the context of marriage. He said, "As the mind goes, the man goes. As the man goes, the woman goes." I fully acknowledge that in this day and age of equal rights, the "me too" movement, women's liberation—and not to mention various social media groups—this type of thinking is viewed as antiquated. Regardless, in my vast experience of working and socializing with men and women of a very diverse socioeconomic status, I can tell you that this "old thinking" is still very much alive and a fully functional part of dating and marriage relationships today. And I don't see it ever changing, at least not for everyday average people. Women want "real men" and men want "real women" to marry or otherwise be in a committed, monogamous relationship.

Men, when you date your wife with intention, you're communicating that she's not only an important part of your life but that she's worthy of your exclusive time, attention, and affection. When she sees this behavior coming from you, you can be assured that she will echo that behavior in the same way and in other ways. It's sort of like the scientific adage, "For every action there is an equal reaction." Dating your spouse is not an obligation. If it feels that way, you need to correct your thinking and get your heart in the right place. It's a necessary component of a healthy, romantic, and generous marriage/relationship. If you allow your attention to become overly focused on your work, your kids, or other extracurricular activities outside the marriage, then it's just a matter of time before some vixen will sense your vibes of unhappiness and use that weakness to swoop in and steal the soul of your marriage.

If you allow your attention to become overly focused on your work, your kids, or other extracurricular activities outside the marriage, then it's just a matter of time before some vixen will sense your vibes of unhappiness and use that weakness to swoop in and steal the soul of your marriage.

Ladies, you're not exempt. The same is true for you. The dark secret of infidelity in marriage is that much of it occurs without a single touch; it happens in the mind and then the heart. Each day it happens you allow yourself to get closer and closer to the fire because its warmth soothes you. The so-called "innocence" offered by flirting or having an online-only relationship is huge in today's technological world. Old high school lovebirds are chatting it up over social media often hundreds of miles apart. The same is true with coworkers, people you know from your kid's football team, your church, or even the cute guy at the local coffee shop you see every week. It can happen so easily and effortlessly that it doesn't even seem like cheating. But it leads to that each time the flame gets a tiny bit hotter, and you get just a little bit closer. What's even more amazing is that it is often permitted in the marriage; that is, the spouse has knowledge and has even granted permission for it to happen online and even in real life. Yup, I'm referring to swinging.

Swinging is easier than ever, and often the opposing spouse gives permission (and/or they give permission to each other) to engage in such activities because they experience a high from it in the context of their own marriage. Believe me, the game of "wife swapping" is alive and well in modern society today and is so more than ever—thanks to texting, specific websites that cater to that specific "subculture," and smartphone apps where you can send pictures and messages—either anonymously or under your real name—and that message quickly disappears after being received and read. Often the "permission" that is granted to the wanting spouse is done so to provide relief of marital obligation to the other spouse. It gives both parties an excuse to work less on the marriage so that one or both of them can be fulfilled in a multitude of ways by another person. At the same time, it simply gives one spouse a break from their partner's sexual desires, meaningful conversation, or they simply enjoy alone time. To be clear, this isn't a one-sided thing in a marriage. Both men and women request permission to engage in this type of thing fairly equally.

Much like the locomotive metaphor, once this train gets moving it's nearly impossible to bring it to an end. When it does come to an end, it's often in divorce. And for the lucky ones—or perhaps the not-so-lucky ones—that survive the devastation of swinging in marriage, it is exponentially difficult to get past once the marriage returns to monogamy. Do yourself and your spouse a huge favor and skip this whole painful and destructive process. Just start dating like you did once upon a time. You were passionately in love before, and you can be again; it just takes time and communication—and understanding each other's love language is a great place to start.

A magnificent date-night topic for a married couple is Dr. Gary Chapman's book *The Five Love Languages*. I have personally read this book more times than any other book in my life. Yes, it's that good. And his teachings are just as applicable to single people as they are for married couples. The book outlines five general "love languages" that couples express and experience heartfelt love and commitment.

The five love languages are described as:

1. Words of Affirmation

2. Quality Time

3. Physical Touch

4. Acts of Service

5. Receiving Gifts

The purpose of my book isn't to delve deeply into these; however, I strongly recommend you read *The Five Love Languages* book as a very suitable pairing to this one.

What I do want to point out is that the type of love language you possess is often the type of love language you project on your significant other. I'm not talking about just your spouse, but others too. It could be your kids, your coworkers, your family, anyone. For example, if you love to do things for people, then it's likely that your love language is acts of service. If you're the type of person that likes to make little care packages to give to people then your love language could be gift giving.

The friction that can occur in a marriage relationship is if your spouse's love language is, for example, words of affirmation, then you can do their laundry, clean their car, even clean the kitchen floor with a toothbrush on your hands and knees, yet your most genuine acts of service will never pierce the most sensitive part of their heartfelt affection for you because you're not speaking their love language. Imagine two people who speak two very different languages sitting at a table and trying to have a conversation. Funny, right? It's also very frustrating and can lead to people giving up on a potentially great relationship too early. But those same two people, when they start with a simple dialogue and build on it continuously and grow closer and closer by understanding each other's love language, then the relationship—and especially the intimacy—can flourish in ways you never imagined.

Generally speaking, there is no dead-on accurate compatibility test between the love languages. I have personally experienced what it's like to be in a meaningful relationship with someone that had the exact same love language as mine, yet the relationship didn't last. You were born with your love language in you and/or it was equally embedded in you starting in your childhood, then into your adulthood years. Just because your spouse doesn't have your identical love language doesn't mean you're not compatible. Date nights are a super great time to talk about each other's love language and how the other person met or exceeded your expectations. Careful, though; this can backfire too. Just because your spouse knows your love language doesn't mean they're going to "speak it" the way you want to receive it all the time. There are other things in their life other than catering to your love language needs on a daily basis—and the same is true for you. Learning and intentionally meeting the expectations of your loved one's love language is about quality and not quantity. Read the book. Make it a topic during an upcoming date night. Expand the love of your marriage in ways you've been dying to try with the person you love more than anyone else on this earth. You won't regret it!

CHAPTER 18

A Season of Solitude - Not Loneliness

A dear friend of mine was going through a difficult divorce when she called me and asked if she could please hang out with me on Christmas Eve. Ugh, my heart was instantly broken for her because I know how this feels. It's that feeling when you've been in a relationship for over two decades and now you're faced with not only being alone but being alone during a major holiday—and especially alone during Christmas when you're used to being surrounded by your kids and family. Like my family, the vast majority of hers lived throughout the country, but in her hometown it was just her, her kids, and her soon-to-be ex-husband. He had the kids on Christmas Eve, and they were going to spend Christmas together with the kids in hopes of at least giving them a sense of normalcy. I remember when I was first divorced and the feeling of utter emotional anguish of being alone anytime, much less on the holidays. Like her, I had gone from nearly two decades of a stable family unit to now not having a wife and seeing my kids only 50 percent of the time. I did so many things to cope. I drank during the week, which was something I had not typically done. I worked longer hours. I worked out more. I dated for all the wrong reasons—and not to mention, I was an emotional train wreck and was not well suited for dating. If this sounds familiar to you, this chapter is specifically for you.

It doesn't matter whether you've been married for decades or just exited a relationship of only a few months, or anything in between; the length of the relationship is irrelevant. What is relevant is the seemingly emotional death of a relationship that was part of your daily life and no longer exists. That empty and lost feeling of loneliness is common, and it is a season that you must endure. You must endure it simply because at the end of the day the sun will still rise. You'll still have a job to go to, bills to pay, and your physical and mental health to tend to. I want to also point out that whether your lost relationship was of your own making or it was something that was done *to* you, the pain experienced is just the same. I would even strongly argue that if you're the one who ended it, that can be especially painful. You gave the other person no choice, but because you made the choice, you might be constantly questioning whether or not you made the right decision in addition to experiencing the heartache. Yes, you probably made the right decision, and for the right reasons. You may even feel better off, but when it's all said and done, a love lost is painful regardless of what caused it.

It's ok to feel lonely; it's normal. Now you must look to the future and embrace this season of solitude, not loneliness. In this season, it is the right time, right now, finally, to be in preparation. I want you to think of all the notable biblical characters, movie stars, big business-successful people, and remember this: They all experienced a season of solitude and embraced it to prepare them for the better and for a bigger and brighter future. I know this is easier said than done. Believe me, I know. As I'm writing this book, I am in that season and have been for some time.

Here are some things I've learned—and it is my heart's deepest desire that my reflections can help you turn the emotional corner and know that your future is bright, prosperous, and will be better than ever. Whether you believe in the Almighty or not, the centuries-old stories of how God prepared his chosen people for his purpose and a higher blessing are worth a notable mention in this chapter. There are so many examples, and the one that I reflect on often is one from a celibate man. Jesus knew he was the son of God, yet he did not begin his ministry until the ripe old age of thirty. He was in solitude and preparing for his purpose for thirty years. He waited. He studied and prayed and learned to be a carpenter. He went about his daily life happily, much the same way you do now.

The ending of the story of Christ's life and ministry is bleak; that is, he was hung on a cross and died—but I would be remiss if I didn't mention that he also rose from the grave and ascended into heaven. As far as mortal death goes, this is not exactly a bad way to go. The point is this: He spent his entire life preparing and embracing his solitude to fulfill his higher purpose.

While we're on the topic of a higher power, if you're experiencing feelings of being punished by God, let me assure you, you are not being punished. God does not punish people; he guides them. Have you ever experienced a sense of great accomplishment and reward for your actions and, at the same time, also reflected on the amount of time and work it took to get there? Was it worth it? In most instances, the answer is, "Yes, it was worth it."

If your answer is "No," then at the least you learned a ton about yourself and what not to do in the future. What doesn't kill ya makes you stronger, right? Absolutely! Those negative experiences now and in the past have made you wiser, stronger, and a much better personal navigator of your life's journey.

So what are you going to do? Are you going to feel sorry for yourself and spend the next few months or, worse yet, years, feeling punished, pouting, and dulling your senses with alcohol, pointless sex, raging resentment, and become the worst cynic the world has ever seen until you spiral yourself into a position of being so undateable that you feel all hope is lost? You know the answer. However, in case you need help, the answer is no, you're not going to do that. You're going to embrace what you've read in this book. You're going to huddle up on the battlefield with yourself, and you're going to press on and thrive.

What you think about expands, and what you think about the most expands the most. It does so in all facets of your life. So why not make the decision today, right now, to put this energy to good use. When you dwell on the loss and loneliness you're experiencing, it makes about as much sense as digging your own grave, lying in it, and pushing the dirt on top of you.

Let me be clear on one very important point: If you're feeling punished and you're heaping up mounds of resentment in your heart and in your thoughts day by day, or even hour by hour, then you're undateable. Once you come to terms with it, you'll realize this isn't a bad thing. This negative energy that is exuding from your soul can be used for good. You must make a choice: Will you channel this energy for good or will you allow it to perpetuate and grow? What you think about expands, and what you think about the most expands the most. It does so in all facets of your life. So why not make the decision today, right now, to put this energy to good use. When you dwell on the loss and loneliness you're experiencing, it makes about as much sense as digging your own grave, lying in it, and pushing the dirt on top of you. That is not your design, it is not your purpose, and it isn't how you want to live and feel. You deserve the very best. It takes work and it takes time. This season of solitude may not be by your design, but during this time you can slingshot yourself ahead in ways you never thought possible. Use this time to reflect and commit to personal growth, career growth, education—or even get in the best shape of your life. Hell, I say do them all! I did!

I want to share something from my personal life that has changed me dramatically and made me a much better person, businessman, and has vastly improved my dateable nature. After my divorce, my attorney—whom I became good friends with (because of this statement)—said to me, "Now Shanks, go figure out who your real friends are." To be honest, when she said it I blew it off as just another piece of advice that I had been hearing for months from countless well-meaning people. But as the months went by and my soul-searching was getting deeper and deeper (not to mention the countless attempts I made to fill my emotional potholes with the wrong things), I began to understand just what she meant and the true intention of her powerful statement.

Something I began noticing for the first time in my life that was always there (but I didn't acknowledge) was that I'm actually a likable person and that there are a multitude of people that wanted to be friends with me that I never engaged. I never engaged because I was always too busy with work or rushing to get home to tend to the family. That was my life then. Now in my season of solitude, I have formed multiple strong friendships with people—not work people either. I mean genuine people that were never a part of my physical or emotional world before. Some of them are girls, some are guys, some are married, some are single, some are older, and some are younger. I have collectively learned so much from all of them, and I've borrowed pieces of their life and my relationship with them to expand my own horizons—as I hope I've done for them. If you are a person that already does this, then high five. I've always been a lone wolf with a workaholic tendency, so this was a whole new world to me. When you do this, you'll find that those lonely nights can easily be filled with healthy friendships where you can go to the local sports bar for a beer and wings, church groups, form a gym family, and even travel. You'll find that you'll be able to do it all with someone, or multiple people, that you can turn to—and they turn to you—for support, good times, and genuine life-changing friendship. You are made for healthy human relationships, and it doesn't have to be a dating relationship for you to feel fulfilled and have a sense of worth or personal fulfillment. I can't stress enough how awesome it is to have a group of friends that you can call or text anytime and get a response. They need you and you need them. Humans are made for community. Our souls are interconnected by a divine design, and in your journey of solitude you will need people that you can call upon when you need them—and they will be able to call you when they need someone. Plus, here's a bonus: The more you have, the easier it is to fill your free time with new activities and learn new things. Collectively, they will become your personal advisors on all things you while you're on this amazing journey of new self-discovery, redefining, and personal growth. What you think about expands, and what you think about the most expands the most. So get out there and expand your social circle so it can expand your life in ways you never thought imaginable. You'll be happier, healthier, and smarter, and you'll have a stronger foundation to build your future intimate relationship on. Have faith in this season of solitude. You'll be rewarded, and you'll look back and know it was all worth it. I promise!

CHAPTER 19

Getting Stood Up!

If you've been in the dating pool long enough, chances are really good that at some point you've been stood up for a date or, worse yet, you've been on a great date (or even several great dates) with the same person, then all of a sudden they disappeared—a term often referred to as being "ghosted." Here's the thing that really sucks about either situation—and I'm speaking not only from my own personal experience, but also from many singles I've talked to while writing this book—the person you're most excited about meeting and dating for whatever reason often ends up being the person that stands you up. Yuck! It happens, and it's completely unrealistic to think that it's not going to affect you personally. You'll struggle with the rejection and spend countless hours talking to yourself—probably out loud—wondering why this wonderful person that you were so excited about dating flat out stood you up.

My first experience with being stood up was with a gal from across state lines that I met on a dating app. We talked very casually and humorously for about a month, and the chemistry was, in a word, perfect! I was stoked out of my mind to finally have a date set for our first date. She was absolutely gorgeous but in a real down-to-earth, country girl kinda way; soft eyes, long hair, perfectly symmetrical from head to toe—and she was smart and a bit feisty. PERFECT! She had a killer sense of humor, and like me, she too was a business owner. We had some great foundational things in common, and in my mind, it was a match made in heaven.

I made reservations at a nice restaurant, got my hair cut, found a sitter, and hell, I even bought a brand new pair of boots. Listen, if a dude buys a new pair of boots to go on a date with you, he's mega serious about making a good impression—maybe a little pathetic too. I'm just being honest. But yes, I did that.

It was a beautiful summer day, and I got to the restaurant an hour early to be sure I could snag us a great table. I wanted something close—but not too close—to the live music, and make everything perfect. I waited outside for her to arrive. We were going to meet for lunch right at 12:00 p.m. I was so overwhelmed with excitement, and even nervous—and I'm not the type that gets nervous. 11:45 a.m., 11:50 a.m., 11:55 a.m., 11:59 a.m., 12:10 p.m., 12:30 p.m. *Ugh! Ok, something must be wrong, Lord, I hope she didn't have a traffic accident.* I was legitimately only thinking about bad things that could have happened to her. For her not to call or text me, it must be bad! My brain was spinning! The last thing I was thinking was that I was getting stood up. The thought never even entered my mind. I called her, texted her, and waited. Waited some more. Finally it hit me, *I'm being stood up.* I checked the socials and finally went to the dating app to send her a message from there. Her profile was gone. *Yup, I'm being stood up. What in Sam Hill; how could this be happening? Who would stand me up?* I was a perfect gentleman the entire time, and I never came off as inappropriate or anything. I went to the bar, drank whiskey and listened to live music for several hours, then went home. Sad story, huh? That's not the last time I got stood up either. But you get the idea. And if that's happened to you, then you know the sinking, sucky feeling you get. If you've been fortunate enough to never have been stood up, keep dating; eventually it'll happen. The only thing worse than being stood up is being ghosted after several dates.

This isn't a long chapter in this book, but it is a big topic. For those whom this scenario applies, I want to assure you of one thing: It's not you; it's them. There is a myriad of reasons a person will stand someone up on a date without so much as a phone call, and in my opinion, none of them are good enough. But because I'm a big ole softy and always try to put a positive spin on things— remember this, you never know what's going on in someone else's life. Life happens to us all.

The girl in the aforementioned story showed up on my social media feed two months later engaged to be married, so not sure what to think about that but "Oh well." Side note, I saw the guy on her post—what was she thinking? Haha. Like I said, "Oh well." If she found her true love, then how can I not be happy for her?

On another occasion when I was stood up, I heard through the grapevine that the poor girl had gotten so nervous that it made her sick, so she simply didn't show up for fear of having a panic attack. See what I mean? You just never know the reason, and it's best just to push on and not let it get to you. If and when it happens to you, don't sweat it. Don't let it get you down and don't dwell on it. Onward and Upward! That person probably did you a huge favor. Take your seat, enjoy the meal, have a glass of wine, and take advantage of some unplanned "me time." Heck, maybe sit at the bar—and who knows, you might just strike up a conversation with someone really worthy of your time.

Next, if you are stood up, and that person later contacts you, then I would definitely give them the benefit of the doubt and simply listen to what they have to say. Adults have kids. People have lives and are on call a lot. People get sick or nervous and just chicken out. If the conversation or text message starts with an apology followed by a legitimate reason for their absence— and they ask for another time—then it's ok to consider it. Trust your gut. I've heard of people that will refuse a second chance no matter what the excuse is, and I also think that's 100 percent ok. It's perfectly fine to have some standards to live by. If that's you, then it's fine. But be open to listening. Sometimes it's not the dog that ate the homework, sometimes it is. Your gut will steer you in the right direction. What I don't recommend you doing is engaging in a tone of frustration. That will get you nothing other than making you even more upset and possibly burning a bridge that could resurface later when the timing and/or the person is in a better place. Never say never! No matter how excited or infatuated you are with this person—or how awesome the chatting was leading up to the date—if they stand you up, there is a reason. And it's not on you; it's on them. And there could be a perfectly legit reason why. Be open minded; yet it's also prudent to have your bullcrap radar beeping and glowing!

I'm leery to share this, but share I must. My personal standard is this: If it's in my calendar, it'll happen without fail. No matter what it is. Therefore, I do hold my date to the same standard. If someone stands me up, I won't go out with them no matter what they say or how earnest their apology is. I interpret that event as a clear sign that the universe doesn't want me to be with that person. It's just what I do, but it doesn't mean that I don't reserve the right to change my mind in the future.

Good luck out there. You are absolutely worthy of the right person's time and full attention.

CHAPTER 20

Willing vs. Worthy

You see, if you want to really prove your worthiness to another person, nothing says it more than your willingness to adapt for them. Put another way, it's the little things that matter!

I have had countless conversations with both men and women about dating and how they feel that they are "worthy" of dating. They can't understand why no one else recognizes it or why the right person just doesn't seem to fall into their life. Many even wonder if it will ever happen. To be certain, I, too, feel that I am worthy of meeting a great person that's perfect for me and that we can enjoy a long-term relationship. Self-confidence in what you have to offer in your dating relationships is very important and a crucial component of successful dating. At the same time, it's the outer wheel in the cog. There is a wheel in the middle of the wheel; and that is, are you "willing" to adapt to another person? Think of it like gears inside of an old-fashioned pocket watch. The little wheels are what turn the bigger wheels. The big wheel in dating is your worthiness. The much smaller, more powerful wheel that really makes the machine go is your willingness. You see, if you want to really prove your worthiness to another person, nothing says it more than your willingness to adapt for them. Put another way, it's the little things that matter!

Having high self-worth and setting your dating standards in accordance with it is what this book is all about; yet at the same time, having perceived self-worth that is too high, unconvincing, or inaccurate is a crippled mentality. I have found many times in talking to singles from all walks of life that their self-worth can be skewed. That is to say, that while we humans are our own worst critics there is something about the world of dating that we often wrongly judge—on the high side—what our own self-worth is to another person.

This cripples one's ability to attract a long-term relationship and leads to an undateable tendency. I could recount a never-ending list of examples. The first few dates are amazing, and the chemistry is perfect. Then a few dates, weeks, or months in when things get serious and the real you and your real life surface, someone's perception of your worthiness to them can dilute to the point that the relationship ends. It can be a vicious cycle and, if not corrected, can repeat itself over and over again. I have found the key to keeping the positive momentum going is to learn how to and be open to adapting to the other person, that is, if it makes sense. Of course, everyone wants this sentiment reciprocated. More often than not, however, it takes one person to take the lead on this, to lead by example.

If your self-worth is realistic and your standards have been met with another person, yet the relationship seems to be dwindling, ask yourself, "What am I willing to change, accept, or compromise on?" This is not only true once a relationship has been established, but is just as true (if not more so) prior to even entering into a long-term relationship. What bad habits do you have that you need to work on? What good habits do you need to implement in your daily life to improve yourself? For example, you can have a great job, be financially secure, have a great vocabulary, an incredible sense of humor, and be very attentive to the other person. But if you're not living healthy, then over time all those other things will matter less. The one thing that you're not working on or paying attention to may drive a wedge in the relationship and/or your ability to attract a dating relationship. Speaking from personal experience, I can say that I've had far more success in dating people that are more adaptable to me than what I've been able to reciprocate. So this is an area of my dating life that I'm working on to this day.

So when it comes to dating, which is the chicken and which is the egg? Is it better to be "worthy" or to be "willing?" In this author's opinion, the person who is willing to adapt is by far much better off in dating and happier when it comes to initiating or sustaining a dating relationship. Imagine your self-worth as a metaphorical box that you live in each day. It has four walls, a floor, and a ceiling. Is there room in your box for another person even if their self-worth is on par with your own? Is this self-worth box you live in perhaps a bit too constrictive? What if you were to just loosen up a bit and allow the walls of that box to expand? Not a lot, but just adding a little more room for yourself to breathe and for another person to occupy that space with you. When you decide that you are willing to do that, what you'll find is that there is more room for the right type of worthy person to fall into your world. Even better, you'll find that there will be more opportunities that all of a sudden enter into your dating world.

––––––

Mr. Perfect All the Time

This guy is magnificent all the time! He's a business owner, tall, well-built, makes healthy life choices, very motivated, adventurous, kind, affectionate, attentive, awesome dad, great ex-husband, available to date, church goer, and a great listener. He's 100 percent independent. All his friends say, "That guy really has his stuff together. He manages a successful business and still does his own landscaping, folds his laundry, cooks for the kids, vacuums, works out five days a week, pays his bills on time, and even has time to ride a Harley on the weekends. He also spends ample time with his kids on their homework, fun outings and projects, and takes his family to church every Sunday. He's built houses, cars, has a college education, great vocabulary, funny as hell, knows how to treat people the right way, can read a room like it's no one's business, adaptive to all walks of life, and he loves Jesus. Sure, he gets stressed sometimes with work and life, but that's anyone, right? He's been a serial dater yet still has not found that perfect Miss Right, his twin flame, to share all aspects of life with." So why is this guy so undateable? How is that even possible? It's because this special man has devoted his life to being "worthy" and hasn't focused enough attention on being "willing" to adapt to the right gal when she entered his life. He has treated adaptability like it's Superman's kryptonite and has avoided it at every turn. His mentality has been that "The right girl will *get me* and adapt to me and my life and be my equal in all regards. If it is to be, then God will see to it."

With tears in my eyes, I confess this amazing man is me.

Above all else, the essential ingredient to shedding your undateable skin is to be willing to adapt your life to another. No matter how amazing you think you are, how independent you've designed your life to be, it will never be enough to make yourself ready for a co-equal until you are willing to surrender yourself to another. Surrendering oneself to another is not about reciprocation; it's a personal choice and requires action. If this sounds like you, then take this moment to take a long, slow, deep breath. In my experience, this is 99 percent of the undateable population today. This idea of surrendering and adapting to another person is the single most difficult and, therefore, most important ingredient to becoming dateable. Ask anyone that's been married for decades!

It's only at the end of yourself that you'll find the new, dateable you. That's what you deserve and what your future mate wants from you. Do you just want to be worthy or do you need to be willing?

When you decide to push out the walls of your perfect box and make a personal choice to create room for another person— and stay consistent with that choice—you'll find that your dating opportunities will not only be higher quality, (because you're working on you and not them), you'll graduate to a new level of relationship enlightenment that overflows into all aspects of your life. Imagine the possibilities in your life that would open up outside just your dating world. Your work will be better. Your income will improve. Your spiritual life will elevate. Your parenting will be better than ever. You'll love people in an unconditional way. It's only at the end of yourself that you'll find the new, dateable you. That's what you deserve and what your future mate wants from you. Do you just want to be worthy or do you need to be willing?

Closing

Many of us are in relationship purgatory, that in-between place where we are deciding whether to date again for personal fulfillment and find that match made in heaven or to remain single. If you are ready to pursue a healthy dating life, then do it with grace and a willing frame of mind. If you've chosen to remain single, then do it with gusto and be proud of your independence. Both are perfect and have life-altering rewards. Remember this about yourself: N.M.N.B. Nothing Missing, Nothing Broke. What that means is that regardless of where you are on the seemingly wide spectrum of dating—or just in your daily life—you are right where you need to be. You are not undateable; you are dateable. You are VERY dateable! This book is just one guide to help steer your thinking and your emotions in the right direction. Have faith that you no longer have to accept that you're frozen in this middle space. Focus on where you're going to, not what you're going through. Whatever it is that you're going through and what drove you to pick up this book and read it, it is your perfect journey. This journey is a mission you're on and not a consequence— nor is it your final destination.

Your journey is here, right now. Everything that is happening in your life is to build your character and make you ready for the perfect mate, and that all starts with healthy dating decisions. You get what you deserve in life. When you choose to be willing to work on improving yourself (in dating as well as in all aspects of your life), you create a new aura around you that is infectious to others and makes you very desirable.

God is THE "waymaker." He has prepared you perfectly for this journey so that He can shape and mold you for His kingdom, for His glory and, at the same time, for your happiness in all relationships. It is often said that the "inner me" is the "enemy." This book and all of its concepts are here to shape and mold your "inner me" so that you can become the best version of your dateable self and stop thinking of yourself as your own worst enemy.

My sisters in love, be willing to heal yourself and make yourself ready for the perfectly imperfect life mate. He's out there searching for you. This man will fill you with joy and complete you in ways you never imagined possible.

My brothers in love, be willing to take the initiative and to lead in your dating relationship. She's out there waiting for you to find her. This woman will be your shining crown and will elevate you to levels in your heart, your mind, your body, and in your daily life beyond your greatest dreams.

Lastly, to all of you who have influenced and blessed my life and inspired me to write this book, I want to say thank you for helping to define who I am in dating and in all areas of my life. I leave you with a verse that has impacted my life since childhood, Proverbs 27:17: "As iron sharpens iron, so shall one sharpen another."

We are all on this dating journey together, and we can and should make each other better.

———

THE END

CPSIA information can be obtained
at www.ICGtesting.com
Printed in the USA
LVHW020903021121
702214LV00010B/373